D0660931

A Springtime's Dream

An Italian Girl's Story

by Anna S. Avella

To Carol Park
Thank you and
Good Bless you

Anna Avella

"Anna Signori Avella" is a pseudonym. The names of all the people and many of the places in this narrative have also been changed. The author has chosen this method in order to spare her children, family, and friends any pain or embarrassment. The words and events in A Springtime's Dream: An Italian Girl's Story are based on the author's true life.

Copyright ©1997 by Anna S. Avella

All rights reserved, including the right to reproduce this work in any form whatsoever without permission in writing, except for brief passages in connection with a review.
For information, write:

Publishing Connections
621 Hampton Highway
Yorktown, VA 23693
757-867-8287

All scripture quotations are taken from the HOLY BIBLE, NEW INTERNATIONAL VERSION®. NIV®. Copyright © 1973, 1978, 1984 by International Bible Society. Used by permission of Zondervan Publishing House. All rights reserved.

Library of Congress Cataloging-in-Publication Data
Avella, Anna S.
A Springtime's dream: An Italian Girls Stroy
Library of Congress Catalog Number: 97-75666
ISBN:09643374-8-7

Printed in the United States of America

*This book is dedicated to
my children and grandchildren*

Contents

Acknowledgments

I am thankful to many people for assisting me with this book. I would like to express special gratitude to:

God,
Thank you for guiding me, helping me to remember the painful past, and restoring my heart and joy. You give me the strength to go on.

My children,
You stuck by me during the good and bad times. You offered support when I needed it. May God bless you.

Rosa, my translator
Thank you for helping me tell my story.

D. Michael McDaniel,
Thank you for preparing the vocal and musical arrangements for "La Nostra Casa."

Chapter 1
Early Childhood

I was born on January 24, 1946, in the city of Palermo, on the island of Sicily, Italy. Palermo extends from the mountains to the Mediterranean Sea. It is a breathtakingly beautiful city, full of mysteries and ancient history. Its overbearing palm trees made me dream of exotic lands. During the summers, the palm trees leave a citrus scent on the skin, mixed with the sweet perfume of orange blossoms and jasmine.

My parents, Aldo and Dora Signori, were an extremely loving couple. My father was a good-looking man of medium height with dark hair and eyes, and a fit body. A modest man, he was unpretentious, and content with what he had. He seldom became angry, but when he did he could really yell! His anger seldom lasted more than five minutes and afterward everything was fine again.

My mother, Dora, was madly in love with Papa. She was happy, well dressed, and very beautiful. At night, before Papa came home, she would put on some lipstick to welcome him. Her light brown hair would be nicely tied up and her blue eyes would shine with happiness. With creamy colored skin and a perfectly oval face, she was the epitome of a Sicilian beauty.

Her comforting spirit made her more beautiful, since she rarely became upset and spoke in a simple yet elegant way. Mama was a friend to all who knew her and could always be counted on to lend a hand.

Papa worked with his father, Tito Signori. My grandfather owned Signori and Sons, very big deli in Palermo, that catered wedding receptions. Grandpa employed all of his sons making sure they were all well paid.

When I was born, my family lived in a very large apartment on Romano Street. It was a very noisy, crowded, and lively street in a wealthy neighborhood. Papa and Mama used to entertain a lot of people at our home, where the most luxurious dinners were served. There was even a woman who came over weekly to help Mama around the house.

My early childhood was truly fine. I felt well loved, happy, and rich! I remember having many dresses. My favorite was a light blue one, made of taffeta. I had lots of felt hats and a white leather purse. Papa bought me many toys and dolls, and I would occasionally fight with my older brother, when he wanted to play with my dolls.

Nevertheless, there was so much love in our house. Papa used to hold me in his arms, tease me, and ask me to repeat over and over how much I loved him. When I finally answered, he would hug me and laugh heartily.

I am the fourth of seven children. The first child born to Mama and Papa was Aurora, a very beautiful girl with black eyes and curly black hair. Aurora grew to be a lovely young lady with a shape that made heads turn. Since she was the oldest, Aurora helped Mama take care of all the children. With her keen sense of authority, she kept us straight and clean. When Aurora combed my curly brown hair, I would often cry as she yelled at me to try to keep me still. When she was finished, she would put a huge ribbon on my hair, smile, and place me in front of a mirror. Then she would kiss me and tell me how pretty I looked.

The second child was my brother Angelo. He was a very shy boy, who preferred to stay to himself. He rarely joined in childhood games or talked to us. Like Aurora, he had black hair and a dark tanned complexion. Next to Angelo was Luigi. He was blonde, almost a redhead, with Mama's blue eyes. Stefano was born after me, he too had blonde hair and blue eyes. After Stefano was Rino, a skinny, dark-haired, sweet-natured boy, who was very attached to Mama.

Lisa was the youngest. I was seven when she was born. Most of us were much older than Lisa. We often treated her as if she were a beautiful doll. Lisa was indeed pretty with dark hair and eyes, but she became a spoiled brat! Everyone always gave in to her wishes. I remember having a beautiful carriage that I used to stroll my favorite doll in. When Lisa would cry, my mother would take the doll out of the carriage and put Lisa in it. Although she was spoiled, I loved Lisa very much and enjoyed playing with her.

I had a lot of friends and we would play together whenever Mama gave me permission to go outside. The streets were safe then, because there were no cars; every now and then a horse and carriage would go by. The carriages were colorful with stories of "Rinaldo in Campo," a legendary Italian hero, painted on them. The horses had many colored feathers on their heads and were decorated with little bells, which would ring whenever they moved. I liked to watch those horses, and I wished for my very own. How I would enjoy riding it!

After Rino, my youngest brother, was born, there were many changes in our family. Grandfather's deli went bankrupt. All of a sudden we were poor. Although Grandpa opened a smaller shop and Papa continued to work with him, things were never the same. We were a very large family and our needs were great. The large banquets were replaced by small family dinners, with barely enough food for everyone.

Meanwhile, I was bubbling with excitement about beginning grade school. Every morning Mama would dress me in a well-ironed, white uniform, and walk me to school. I was shy and rather tiny for my age, but my friend, Pippo, who was tall and fat, would look after me. My first grade teacher, Miss Rosalia, was a beautiful young woman who made learning fun.

One day while climbing the stairs to our apartment, an angel appeared before me. He was dressed in white with two big white wings, and he was holding a jewelry box in his right hand. He said, "Anna, if you're good, you will have a gift." I looked around, scared and nervous, but somehow I understood that it was not a jewel I was being shown, but something special! The angel said nothing else and as quickly as he appeared, he disappeared. Excited, I ran to tell Mama and all the others. But everyone laughed at me, thinking it was just the overactive imagination of a seven year old. Only Mama believed me.

One summer afternoon, Mama gave me permission to go outside to play, but I could not find any friends to play with. I was so disappointed, while sitting alone on the steps in front of our apartment. As I looked around for a familiar face, I saw a man sitting on the steps to the left of me. He had on a dark red robe with a light blue sash across his chest, and he wore brown sandals. He did not say a word, we spoke with our eyes. Then I arose and we played a game with small stones, laughing as we played together. Then as suddenly as he had appeared, he was gone. I knew it was Jesus! I had had another divine experience.

I ran upstairs to tell Mama, who began to cry. After these heavenly visitations, I would often find Mama crying. I later found out that some people believe if you have a heavenly visitation you are going to die.

Meanwhile, I was so excited I decided to become a nun. I began going to the Catholic Church every Sunday. There I met Sister Maria, a nun, and became very attached to her. She was a sweet lady and I told her all about the angel and my desire to become a nun. She invited me to go to the convent on Sunday afternoons, where she taught me catechism. I studied so hard that year I received a gold medal, after coming in first place in a religious competition.

As time went by, the poverty we suffered became unbearable. Our apartment was repossessed and we were forced to live with my maternal grandparents. We cried so much. Our apartment was full of happy memories. My brother, Luigi, cried hysterically trying to convince Mama to let us keep our tabby cat. Mama kept saying there was no room for a cat, but she gave in to calm Luigi down. We were so happy to be allowed to keep our cat.

My grandparents' house was surrounded by gardens. There were many fruit trees, even prickly pear trees, and many colorful flowers! The house had a large dining room. At night it became our bedroom, and what a bedroom! It was about five hundred square feet in size and easily stored the four foldup beds my siblings and I shared, as well as Mama and Papa's large bed.

Grandma Anna was a very nice lady, but she wanted everything kept spotless. Grandma would complain when we broke any of her flowers, while playing in the gardens around her house. Grandpa Toto was nice too. He was a small man, but had a very authoritative presence that kept us all in line. Mama said he was a descendant of royalty.

We all attended school, except my sister Aurora, who was already engaged to be married. I was one of the best students in my third grade class. Two other students and I, won a trip around Sicily. We were received by the president of Sicily and were each awarded diplomas, which recognized our academic achievement. The ceremony took place at the Villa D'Orleans, next to the president's house. Mama and Papa were very proud of me, and Mama accompanied me on the bus that carried me and the other kids around Sicily. What a memorable experience!

My favorite refuge was still the convent of San Paolo. Many afternoons I went there to meet Sister Maria and all the other nuns, who were growing attached to me. Sister Maria taught me how to sew and always gave me things to bring back to my family. I was very happy to be within those sacred walls. The convent was located in Piazza Camporeale and it was a huge building that belonged to the prince of

Italy. It had a very large garden lined with palm, peach, and pear trees.

In the middle of the garden stood a cave with a running waterfall, and a statue of the Holy Mary inside. The floors of the convent were made of wood and had drawings of flowers carved in them. The ceiling was adorned with drawings of flowers also. On the top floor there was a large atrium with a glass floor, which had drawings of flowers against a royal blue background. There was also a chapel of indescribable beauty. It was made entirely of gold, and was filled with religious paintings and decorations. I would often hide and pray in the chapel; it was such a peaceful place.

During the summers, Mama sent me to day camps. In the morning a military truck would pick up children throughout Palermo to take us to camp. Usually, the camp was held in an old castle at the top of a mountain. The castle was called the Uttivaggio, and the mountain was Monte Pellegrino. We drove for about a half hour to get to the top of Monte Pellegrino, where the castle stood. The bright pink castle was majestic and could be seen throughout the city. I enjoyed the peaceful surroundings on the mountain. I would often take long walks amongst the sweet smelling pine trees.

Since I was very shy, it was difficult for me to make friends. So I learned to weave bracelets and necklaces from pine branches, and participated in acting classes. I knew my family would come and watch my little play, and Mama would be happy to see me acting. Every afternoon the camp counselors would give us a snack, but I did not eat mine. When the military truck brought me back home, I would give my snack to an old beggar who sat on the street corner near my grandparents' house. This generous act made me feel very happy.

After living in my grandparents' house for two years, more changes started taking place. First, Aurora and her fiancee, Emilio, set their wedding date for November 25,

1957. Then my father's parents gave us an apartment in one of their apartment buildings. The new apartment was not too far from our old house. It was located on Riscossa Street in a new development. The neighborhood was growing and was surrounded by big, new houses.

Around the neighborhood there were pastures, and I would often watch sheep grazing. Mama would buy fresh milk from the shepherds, because there were no stores around. Our apartment was on the first floor and it had four large rooms plus a kitchen, bathroom, and a small terrace with a staircase that led to a garden below.

In the garden there were several plum, pomegranate and orange trees. Their blossoms smelled so sweetly. There was also a big, green jasmine bush that circled the balcony. I really liked the new apartment. It seemed like a palace compared to my grandparents dining room. I had the smallest room, which I shared with Aurora until she married.

It was now September 1957, and my sister's wedding was planned for November. The months were mixed with preparations and worries because Mama and Papa had little money to help pay for Aurora's wedding. Yet Aurora was still very happy.

I was a bit nervous because once Aurora was married, it would be my turn to take care of all the younger children. I was only eleven years old and already faced with the sadness of having to quit school, because Papa did not have the money to buy my books. I liked school and was such a good student.

When my teacher found out I was being taken out of school, she came to my house to beg my parents to allow me to return. She cried when my mother told her that I could no longer go. She was an elderly, large woman who cared very much for me. When she left, she took some of my notebooks as keepsakes.

Aurora's wedding day finally arrived. There was so much

confusion in our house that morning. All of my brothers were fighting over who was going to take a bath first. Papa was the first to get ready. He was moved when the photographer arrived, and everyone was ready. My sister was beautiful in her white lace wedding gown. Her black eyes were shining with joy. Our family was so happy for her. Mama was dressed in a brown dress and coat and Papa wore a black suit. My dress was beige and I wore matching beige shoes.

The wedding ceremony was lovely and occurred right on schedule. The only thing that brought sadness to the bride and groom was that Emilio's grandmother was not there. She had suffered a stroke the day before the wedding, and died the next day.

Aurora's marriage meant new chores for me. I now had to do the washing, which I did by hand, and clean the house. I also started taking sewing lessons to learn how to design and make clothes. And, whenever I could, I went to visit Sister Maria. I would go to the chapel and pray, which gave me the strength to return home and face the day's work.

Surprisingly, the first year went by very fast. I found myself taking on more and more household responsibilities to help Mama. There were four boys plus Papa to take care of and Mama, who had fallen down and broken an arm, could not do it all. My little sister, Lisa, was five and too young to be of much help. So I worked hard. I did it willingly and even began to sing while I worked. My cousin Romina would often come to keep me company, and we would listen to music and dance.

Luigi was the only one I did not like to take care of. He was fifteen and seemed to grow more obnoxious everyday. He was the problem child for my poor parents. Angelo, who was now twenty, was drafted into the Italian Army. He only came home a few times to visit. I was close to Angelo and really missed him a lot. Stefano, who was ten, always wanted to play. Rino, who was eight, clung to Mama's apron, and Lisa was the most spoiled of them all.

One thing that never seemed to change was our extreme poverty. It was really bad; we often had nothing to eat! Mama would become resourceful and make some flour fritters, a sugarcoated fried dough, or bread soup. Papa would go to little towns fairs around Palermo to set up tents, where he sold sandwiches to earn money. The days when he worked at the fairs were memorable. He would come home late at night and wake us all up to eat ice cream! In the morning he and Mama would go grocery shopping, and we would have real food. At least for one day we would have a dinner worthy of a king, complete with dessert and ice cream!

On several of these occasions, we even went to a restaurant in a nearby town called, Mondello. It was a beautiful, wooded sea resort on the beach. The restaurant had a terrace overlooking the water and we would sit there and watch the Mediterranean Sea with its splendid, blue waters. It was one of the most breathtaking, picture-perfect nature scenes. Papa and Mama would often look one another in the eyes, as if falling in love all over again.

Meanwhile Aurora gave birth to her first child, a boy, whom she named Roberto. Whenever they came to visit, I was so excited about holding Roberto. What a bundle of joy! It felt so important to be an aunt.

The winter of 1958 was really hard for my family. Papa was working, but the money that he made was not enough for such a large family. Poor little Papa! It was a horrible position to be in. He felt bad about our circumstances, and would always ask us if we loved him to the point of tiring us.

Chapter 2
A Springtime's Dream

My job of taking care of the house was getting harder every day. I liked taking care of the garden though, and I always planted new flowers in pots to decorate the stairway. How I admired their beauty!

One day while working in the garden, I looked towards the stairs and saw the most handsome young man! He was tall and athletic, with classic features, dark hair and two huge green eyes; the quintessential Italian man. When I spotted him, he was chatting with a woman on the terrace of an apartment building around the corner, that faced my backyard. Our eyes met and we kept staring at each other, as if in a trance. It was the Spring of 1959 and I was thirteen years old.

The garden was in full bloom, and the air was filled with many floral scents. I thought I was having a vision. I had always pictured one of these perfect encounters! But fortunately, it was not a vision. The next day I saw him again, and my heart was trembling just at the sight of him. Thus, the seeds of a love story were planted. I forgot all about wanting to become a nun. Instead, I began to fantasize about that handsome, young face.

Every day, whenever I had a little time, I would run to the window of my room which overlooked the garden hoping to see him. I noticed that he did the same thing! We would only stare at each other, never uttering a word. I did not even know his name, but I knew I loved him.

One day with the excuse of putting the clothes out to dry, something that Mama usually did, I went into the garden and finally heard his mother call his name. It was Bruno. His name sounded so sweet to my ears, especially since I was falling in love with him.

He would often stare at me too, but he never said a word! Soon we added music to our eye communication. I liked to sing, so if I wanted to send him a message, I would sing a song with the words of my message. He did the same, and I was content. Nothing bothered me anymore, neither poverty, nor too much house work. I did everything happily, knowing that in any free moment I would be able to see my love. His eyes always looked for mine, and his voice was so melodious. It was music to my ears and heart. I had no idea of his age. I guessed he was around eighteen or twenty, because he was well built.

Bruno's apartment was still under construction. When it was finished his entire family moved into the neighborhood. He often sat on the balcony playing his guitar. I listened to him in ecstasy. In the meantime I had finished my sewing lessons and began making clothes for myself. During the summer months, I would bring the sewing machine onto the terrace feeling so close to Bruno, as he sat on his balcony playing the guitar.

A year after Bruno moved in, Mama had major surgery. She had a hernia and appendicitis, and it nearly killed her. Thank God her surgery went well. After the operation she was hospitalized for about a month. I was left to take care of the house and my brothers and sisters. I was really scared for Mama. I did not want her to die. During the time that she was recovering, I did my best to keep the household running. I cleaned, cooked, washed, and ironed. Yet everyday I found time to visit Mama in the hospital. Aurora also helped, but it was harder for her because of her baby, Roberto. One afternoon while coming back from the hospital, Bruno's mother stopped me to ask how my mother was doing. She seemed very interested in me, and it made my whole day.

To the great relief of our family, Mama finally came

home. She had lost a lot of weight and her face was so pale, but little by little she regained her strength. Aurora would spend the whole day at our house and leave at night with her husband, Emilio. The house was full of commotion. Throughout this hectic time, which lasted about a month, I had no time to think of Bruno.

When Mama was completely well, I had more time for myself. Bruno started talking to me, and his voice made me so happy. I found out he was only eight months older than me. I could hardly believe it! He seemed so mature. Our love grew stronger every day, and I had this overwhelming desire to hold his hand and to go for long walks with him. However, we had to be content with looking at each other and dedicating songs to each other. Bruno began working as a waiter at a large cafe called Cafe del Corso, located in downtown Palermo, so we only sang to each other at night.

In the winter of 1960, I met two girls, Rita and Rosetta, who lived nearby. We became good friends and spent hours chatting, sharing our dreams. We would take walks together. Rosetta would not go out with us as often, because her father would not allow her to leave the house but she was allowed to come and visit me. Rosetta would talk to my mother and always tell me how lucky I was to have such a sweet and understanding mother. Rosetta would often speak highly of her brother Vito. However, I did not meet him, because he was rarely at home.

After a few months Rosetta and I began working at a tailor's shop in the neighborhood. The tailor was Mrs. Morello, a very cheery lady. We worked for her from morning to late evening and earned a quarter a day. The main topic of our conversations was usually boys. Rosetta had a boyfriend too, but they were not serious. On the contrary, I could not wait to go home and see Bruno sitting on his balcony playing his guitar.

Time seemed to fly, everything was so romantic and beautiful. It was summer again, and in my garden the flowers were so many and splendid. The jasmine flower had the strongest perfume. It could be smelled throughout the house and garden.

After eating dinner and helping Mama with the house cleaning, I would have a little time to go onto the terrace and chat with Bruno. We were madly in love. Every night I would wait until everyone was in bed, then I would sneak out to the terrace. Bruno would be waiting for me, and we would talk for hours. We would talk to each other through a wall made of ivy, which enabled Bruno to hear me but he could not see me. I would laugh and tease him. The moon even seemed to look and smile down upon us.

We talked about so many things. Our mothers knew about our relationship and were both supportive. I was now fifteen and Bruno sixteen. Too young to court, but it did not matter. We were willing to wait, as long as necessary, because we loved each other so.

In January 1961, Rosetta invited me to Vito's eighteenth birthday party. By now, I had met Vito. Almost every Sunday my friends and I would hang around or dance at my house or Rosetta's. My brother Angelo, who had returned from the military and found a job in Palermo, was usually my escort. Mama would never let me go anywhere without Angelo.

Angelo escorted me to Vito's birthday party, where there were about a dozen young people. Everyone was happy and Vito, who had always been kind to me, was the happiest of all. He appeared to be a very nice young man and was very good looking. He was not very tall, but had the most gorgeous hair, and light brown eyes. He even had dimples in his cheeks. He was rather skinny, but had a good sense of humor. Vito made a good friend.

That night, Vito kept staring at me and asked me to dance several times. While we were dancing, he told me that he had loved me from the first day we met. I was stunned. I did not know what to do or say. I had no idea he had feelings for me. Nevertheless, I was already in love, so I said, "I am sorry. You are a great friend, but I love someone else. If you want, you can be my friend or we can forget that too, and I will never call your sister again."

Vito was infuriated. He didn't even answer me. He just walked away and went into another room. A little while later he came back and said, "I am sorry, Anna, I want to be your friend. I promise I will never bring this up again. Please forgive me and let's keep on being friends."

Slowly our group of friends grew into a very harmonious and coherent group that included Rosetta, her sister Ella, my cousin Romina, Romina's brother, Carlo, Vito, Angelo, and me. Vito kept his promise and never mentioned anything else about his feelings for me. All was well with Bruno. We both worked and could be together only at night at our ivy wall.

One day we decided to meet face to face. Naturally I said nothing to my mother, because I knew at fifteen I was too young to date. The only time Bruno and I could meet was on Sundays, when we went to church. Since I walked to church with my cousin Romina, I confided in her. She was very supportive of our date and promised to cover for me. When the fateful day came, I was nervous. I got dressed very carefully in a white skirt and a light blue blouse with white print. It was not an expensive outfit, but I liked it a lot. When I came outside, Bruno was already waiting for me, and while Romina continued to walk to church, I walked away with Bruno.

We held hands and were both so nervous, we could not even talk. But being able to hold hands and be near each other was like a dream come true. We did not need to talk! He gave me a box of chocolates and a record featuring the latest hit of Nico Fidenco, a popular singer. We both liked his songs. Everything was going perfectly. Then suddenly Bruno looked upset and scared. I looked up and saw his father walking straight towards us, and it was too late to change route! I felt so embarrassed and upset. What could I do? What could I say? Nothing of course. When his father reached us, he told Bruno to leave, but sweetly apologized to me.

I went back home full of fear, hoping that Mama would not find out. Papa would have been angry and yelled at her for allowing me to go out with Bruno. When I arrived home, I hid the chocolates and record, and started helping Mama prepare dinner. After dinner I went into the garden and found Bruno already on his balcony waiting for me. He threw me a letter attached to a clothes pin. With his eyes he assured me that everything would be fine. His letter indicated that his father would talk to my father and, according to the customs of the days, there would be an official engagement between us. We could then talk to each other freely, but not meet alone. Reading his note made my whole day, as I recalled how wonderful it had been to be with him.

That same afternoon Uncle Peppino, Mama's brother, came to visit. Uncle Peppino did not come too often, and when I saw him coming I was grew scared, afraid he was going to tell my parents that I had been seen alone with Bruno. Fortunately Papa was not home, but he did tell Mama that Bruno was in love with me and that his father would soon come and speak with Papa. Uncle Peppino knew Bruno's family very well. His wife, Aunt Paolina, and Bruno's mother were cousins.

Mama did not find out about our evening chats at the ivy wall, so they continued. We did not dare meet outside of that, although we longed to be together. The hardest part would be getting through the fall months. I would turn sixteen in January and Bruno would be allowed to come to my house for visits. Everything seemed perfect, and I never thought anything or anyone could ever come between us. As I fantasized about life with Bruno, I was sure my life would be like a beautiful springtime dream.

One spring day I received a letter from Vito. While reading it, my heart jumped to my throat, and I began to cry. In his letter Vito again declared his love for me. If I cont-inued to reject his love, he said he would commit suicide. Those thoughts started to obscure my mind. Vito was a dear friend, and I cared for him as a friend, but nothing more. I truly loved Bruno. How could I say yes to him? What could I do? It was a tragic situation. And what if Vito really did kill himself? Would I be left with that guilt for the rest of my life? These questions were torturing me. I had no answers. I cried desperately for hours with no one to talk to.

When Mama came home and found me crying, she demanded to know why. I never was good at hiding anything from Mama, so I showed her the letter. Mama looked me in the eyes and said, "Anna, tell me the truth, what is it that you want to do?" I answered, "I love Bruno. I can't say yes. Vito is only a friend to me." Mama took the letter in her hands and went to Vito's house to talk to his parents. When she came back, she warned me severely to break off this friendship and she said she would not let me go to anymore parties. I agreed to do as she said, but told her I still wanted to be friends with Rosetta.

Angelo and Vito were close friends. Whenever Vito came to visit him, I would say hello and go to a different room. My brother-in-law, Emilio, was also a friend of Vito. My mother and I never told any of them what had happened. Everything continued as usual, but I always found an excuse not to go to any more parties. Whenever Vito met me, he would look at me with pleading eyes. It made me sad to see him suffering, but what could I do?

Aurora was now expecting her second child. And in the eighth month of her pregnancy, she fell down a ladder while hanging some drapes. She was very ill, and although she did not lose the baby, she had to spend the last month of her pregnancy in bed. Mama had to help her, and I had to move in with Aurora to take care of the baby and help around the house. For a whole month, I did not see Bruno. I could not wait until I could go back home. A couple of days before the delivery, my brother-in-law, Emilio, and Mama decided to bring Aurora to our house. I was happy, finally I could see Bruno again.

Aurora gave birth to another son, Aldo, a beautiful baby in perfectly good health. He was born at our house, and I remember the minute I heard his cry, after hours of waiting in my room. Oh, the joy I felt, when my mother brought the baby to my room wrapped in a towel. I fell asleep smiling.

Household chores continued to increase. There was so much work to do, my little nephew, Roberto, to take care of, but the nights were for mine. It was August and in the evening, as usual, I would slowly get up and sneak out onto the terrace to my ivy wall. Bruno was always so sweet, and whenever his mother called him, he would always beg for five more minutes. We could not stop talking and dreaming; we were so happy.

A month after Aldo's birth, the family decided to baptize him and have a little party at our house. The day before the party, I found out that Emilio had invited Vito. What could I do? To avoid any problems, I decided that I wouldn't dance with Vito. That evening I shared my plan with Bruno. He knew all about Vito's infatuation with me, because I never kept anything from him.

I was totally shocked when Bruno responded, "If Vito comes to the party, you will never see my face again." I tried to convince him that it was out of my hands. I promised not to dance with Vito. Bruno knew I did not care for Vito, but he was out of his wits. I felt offended. Why didn't he trust me? Hadn't I shown him love throughout these last years?

During the party, I did not dance with Vito. He asked me

several times, but I refused. I didn't dance at all. I was looking forward to the end of the party so I could return to the terrace to meet Bruno. When that moment arrived, I ran to the terrace, but Bruno was not waiting on his balcony for me. I thought perhaps it was too late, and he had already gone to bed. That night was very, very sad for me.

The day after Aldo's baptism, I thought for sure that Bruno would come to his senses, he would ask my forgiveness and everything would be as before. Boy was I wrong! I spent the entire day hoping to see Bruno. At night I returned to the ivy wall on the terrace, but again, he was not there. I felt the fates had played a cruel joke on me, and all my dreams had been crushed.

The following days were torture. I spent hours in the garden, day and night. I was desperate. I loved him so much! How could it have ended? One day, I decided to take matters in my own hands, and with little Aldo in my arms, I went to the terrace and started shouting: "Bruno! Bruno! Bruno!"

No one answered, but after about an half hour there was a knock at the door. When I answered, Bruno's little brother said, "Miss Anna," and handed me a letter. Full of joy and shaking nervously, I opened the letter. I was sure Bruno was coming back to me, but when I read it I was astounded. There was a picture of me attached to a note. In the note, Bruno demanded that I stop calling him, because I was not worthy of him. His words wounded my heart. Were these really my Bruno's words? But why? What had I done?

I could not get over him. I could not accept the end of our love and yet, I had to. I was really sad. I was not eating, or sleeping at night. Mama was suffering too. It hurt her to see me in that condition, and she kept trying to comfort me. Every morning at eight o'clock I always ran to my window, just to catch a glimpse of Bruno walking by. At night, I would do the same, waiting for him to come back from work. Then I would stare out of my window, hoping to see him. But Bruno was gone forever.

January 1962 arrived. My sixteenth birthday was on the twenty-fourth. It was the birthday Bruno and I had waited for. I even saw him that day, but to no avail. Instead of a day of rejoicing and celebration, I was full of grief and sadness. I cried the whole day, especially when I heard a song playing on the radio called "Sixteen Years" sang by Nunzio Gallo. That song just broke my heart, and I cried even more. I began to keep a journal and every night I wrote my deepest feelings, recounting every moment I had shared with Bruno.

Every night Mama came to my room to say good night. She always found me writing. We were very close and she tried to be more understanding and sweeter than ever. She was always my best friend. Whenever I had time, I would also go visit Sister Maria and spend time praying in the chapel of the convent.

Summer was approaching, and Mama thought I needed to get over Bruno. She was tired of seeing me in so much pain, so she decided to send me to spend some time with her brother, Giacomo. My Aunt Aurora decided to send my cousin Romina. So Romina and I started getting ready for our trip. I made some new dresses for myself and one for Romina. In June, Uncle Giacomo came to pick us up and we left Palermo for Capaci, a small town along the Mediterranean Sea.

It wasn't a long trip, about an hour on the train. We had a chance to see such a beautiful environment. The calm, blue sea and the many pretty trees, especially the red and white oleander along the highway. The sight of the sea followed us all the way to the house. Aunt Pia was waiting for us with a wonderful dinner she had prepared. My little cousins were so excited to see us. They welcomed us with so much love, especially Uncle Giacomo who was very funny and made us laugh a lot.

Capaci was very picturesque, with cobblestone streets, all on steep hills overlooking the sea. We had to get used to walking on those cobblestone streets. Oleander trees were everywhere and they were all in full bloom. There was a big church in the middle of the town, and one main street with some shops. The beaches were deserted and beautiful, and the smell of the sea penetrated every room of the house. From the terrace of the house one could see the Mediterranean Sea.

Everyday we went to the beach and took with us a little snack. Uncle Giacomo tried really hard to teach us how to swim. Romina learned fast, but I was only able to tread water after a long attempt. Whenever I was in the shallow water, I would put my head under water and think, "God, please let me forget Bruno. I want to forget him!" But then, when I was laying on the sand, I would write "I love you, Bruno."

I got really attached to Romina as we spent so much time together. Romina was also sixteen, and we had so much in common, mainly broken hearts from love delusions. I began to relax and even to have some fun. My uncle's house had two floors, but it was small. On the first floor was a large bedroom where Uncle Giacomo and Aunt Pia slept, and a small one where my cousins slept. There was also a little bathroom. On the second floor there was a large kitchen and a terrace. Romina and I slept in the kitchen. Sometimes when it was unbearably hot, we would sleep on the terrace, which never bothered anyone.

We had a good time and really enjoyed their home. We talked freely about our broken hearts. One night when there was a full moon, Romina and I decided to play a game. We would both look toward the moon and chant: "Oh dear moon, let me sleep and dream of the man whom I will marry!" After that we went to sleep happily waiting for our dreams. When we woke up, I asked Romina what she had dreamed, and she said that she had dreamed about someone she did not know. I, on the other hand, was furious and upset. I told Romina I did not like the stupid game, because I had dreamed about Vito. Vito, of all people, the cause of all my problems! Romina decided we should repeat the same game for at least two more nights. Romina did not dream about anyone, but I kept dreaming about Vito. We decided it was just a stupid game, and stopped.

We made some friends in Capaci. At night we would go for long walks on Main Street and go for an ice cream, or walk on the beach. The water was so clear and transparent that we could see little fish and octopuses swimming around. We helped our aunt somewhat, but we had fun all day long. Aunt Pia and Uncle Giacomo would always go along with us, but it was okay, because they were truly fun people.

The three months went by really fast, and soon it was time to return home. We were very tanned and healthy looking. Our mothers were happy to see us happy and to know our hearts had mended. I had not completely forgotten my Bruno, but I had gotten over him a little.

I began to work again at Mrs. Morello's shop. Rosetta also worked with me. She had fallen in love with Carlo, a young man from our old clique, and had a lot to tell me. However, she never talked about Vito. My home life was going smoothly. Stefano was fourteen and had begun working at a vocational school. Angelo had a job too, and at least once a week he took me to see a movie. He would walk with me very closely, and none dared look at me. Luigi, who was nineteen, had not found any kind of work and surrounded himself with a bunch of losers. He began getting into all sorts of troubles and made my parents very miserable. There was no longer peace in my family, and Mama was really sad.

Chapter 3
Happy at Any Cost

A couple of weeks had gone by since I returned from my vacation. I resumed my life and did not see Bruno at all. He never came out to the balcony. I would often go to my terrace hoping to catch a glimpse of him, and my heart, still not fully mended, would ache. At night I would vent in my diary and would think back over what had happened. I was convinced that Bruno had never loved me the way I had loved him. Otherwise he would not have left me over such a stupid misunderstanding. Deep in my heart I would always have a little hope that he would come back to me.

One month passed, and I saw Vito again. Immediately he approached me to tell me he still loved me. "I would be happy if you would return my love," he said. Rosetta told him I had broken up with Bruno, so he decided to try his luck again. I did not know what to say. I finally told him that I needed time to think; and that's what I did. I thought and I thought. I spoke to Mama, and she suggested that I think through everything very well before giving him an answer.

I began to think that I was a stupid to still be infatuated with Bruno. Surely he did not love me. On the other hand, Vito had been waiting for me. He had loved me for several years now. So I decided to accept his love. When I told Vito my decision, he was elated and vowed to try to make me happy. He was full of kindness, always paying close attention to me. He was not as eloquent as Bruno and did not say romantic things, but he looked at me with loving eyes, which made me happy.

We started our Sunday night socials, and finally Vito came to my house and asked my father for my hand. Papa was happy because he liked Vito, who was a hardworking young man. He worked in a deli, night and day. After Papa agreed to allow Vito to marry me, his parents came over to discuss a formal engagement.

On January 12, 1963, Vito's twentieth birthday, we had our engagement party at my house. For the occasion I had made a pretty dress. It was dark red and very elegant. Vito also looked sharp in his dark blue suit and was so happy! As was the custom, he brought me a beautiful bouquet of long-stemmed red roses and a little gondola. Inside the box was an engagement ring. It was an Italian custom for a man to hide his fiancee's ring inside a little gift. I admired the ring, as Vito slipped it on my finger. He then held my hand tightly. The engagement party was a huge success and everyone was happy for us. On January 24, I turned seventeen.

Vito was allowed to visit me every evening. He continuously spoke about our future, and I began to fall in love with him. But I realized that we did not share the same ideals. In fact we had many differences. Vito was outgoing and liked to be around a lot of people, while I was more re-served preferring the simple things in life. I would often think about Bruno and how similar we were. It seemed we had been made for one another. I never shared my thoughts about Bruno with Vito, because I did not want to hurt his feelings.

Whenever I saw Bruno, he totally ignored me. Out of spite he would sit on the balcony and sing our songs, which tortured me. I still fantasized about him returning my love, but nothing changed. A few months later, I found out that Bruno had joined the Italian Navy and would be gone for at least two years. I was sad, but at the same time I could now dedicate all my thoughts to Vito.

Soon after the engagement party, I left Mrs. Morello's

shop and went to work at a clothing factory. I earned a bit more money, and I started buying things that I would need for my wedding.

As time went on, I got to know Vito better. Vito said he loved me, but he also liked to go out alone and that would make me mad. Twice we broke off the engagement due to my dislike of this annoying habit. The second time I broke off the engagement, and was feeling relieved and happy. We had been engaged for three years, and many well-meaning family members and friends started meddling in our relationship, trying to help us patch things up. My Uncle Ciccio was so persistent in trying to persuade me to marry Vito.

I felt that my will was totally worthless. In those days when a girl broke her engagement off, she had little chance of meeting other men. So everybody convinced me to stay with Vito. They assured me that he loved me and that all our problems would be worked out in time. Mama would always tell me to be careful, but at the same time she was convinced that Vito loved me and she was happy.

Unsettled by my threat to break off the engagement, Vito began to behave better. We decided to get married the coming year. Again serenity returned to my family, but it would not last long.

In 1966 Luigi and some of his friends were caught stealing. He was facing four years in jail. Papa was brokenhearted. He did not have much money to pay for lawyers. Mama was devastated and cried her heart out. A bitter life began for my parents. Every week Mama would go to the jail to bring Luigi clean clothes, and a care package. It was such a shame for all of us, that we almost refused to go outside. Papa would visit Luigi whenever he could; my siblings and I rarely went.

I had begun to despise Luigi. He had been very mean to me, which made my home life miserable. If I dared argue with him, he would hit me! What I hated the most were the times when he would yell at Mama. He made her cry so many times, I could not stand him! When I would defend Mama, he would yell at me too. A night when Vito came to visit, they would argue, and Luigi would try to chase Vito out of the house. Luigi's wild behavior had gone on for years, and we were all tired of it. So his arrest was indeed a shame but, in a way, a liberation.

After Luigi's arrest, there were many other changes in my house. My brother Angelo had gotten engaged to Tina, and Stefano, who had grown into a good-looking lad, was engaged to a girl named Ninetta. There were three of us engaged simultaneously, but I was the first to marry. Meanwhile Aurora had yet another son. She was now the mother of Roberto, Aldo, and Carlo. Rino was growing taller and was skinny, and even the baby of the family Lisa was now fourteen. With all my wedding preparations I had little time to think about Bruno, but I still hoped that he would find out that I was getting married.

Vito and I decided to get married on January 12, 1967, which was Vito's twenty-fourth birthday. My parents were opposed to the date, hoping we would wait for Luigi's release from jail. But we refused to put our plans on hold for Luigi. Mama was especially sad about our decision, but she soon gave in.

The year 1966 was full of unpleasantness, but there were also the exciting preparations for the wedding. Papa could not give me any financial help at all, so I worked overtime and tried to save as much as possible. At the end of the month I would go shopping with Mama. She would not use any of my money, instead she gave me money for my bus ticket, which I saved. There was a coke machine at the factory where I worked. Everybody sipped cokes as they worked, but I would drink water to save that money too.

The factory owner, Mr. Poitano, was a very nice man and he was very fond of me. I made many friends there, especially a young girl named Lia, who also was saving money for her wedding. Her wedding date was set four months before mine, so we would talk about the progress of each other preparations. In the meantime, Romina also had gotten engaged to a very handsome, blue-eyed young man, named Enzo.

Rosetta, Vito's sister, was my best friend, and she confided in my mother a lot. She had become engaged to Carlo, and they were married before Vito and I.

My wedding day was slowly approaching, only five months away. One day Mama decided to wash and prepare all the linen from the hope chest before the end of the summer. As I went with her, I got the biggest surprise of my life. When we started pulling the boxes out of the hope chest, we discovered that they were all empty! It did not take long for us to figure out what had happened. Luigi had stolen everything and sold them.

My desperation was enormous. What would I do now? I could not afford to replace all the things that I had bought with my life savings. Before the wedding I tried to buy a few things, but it was way too late to try to save money now. Finally Papa, Mama, Vito, and I reached an arrangement. Papa would buy our bedroom furniture and pay for half of the reception expenses. Vito would pay for the dining room furniture and the other half of the reception expenses. Vito and I would save for our honeymoon.

As the wedding drew nearer, I began to panic. But then I would notice how much Vito loved me and calm down. My Aunt Lia offered to sew my wedding dress as a present, but I still had to buy all the materials. I made my honeymoon clothes at night, after I got home from work. Everything was ready except the veil. But Mama had no money to offer, she had to buy clothes for everybody else.

Two months before the wedding Vito lost his job and started working at Caprera, a deli. That job did not last very long either. We had already rented a little apartment and we were therefore very confused. Luckily Vito got his job back at Caprera, bringing joy to everyone. I was dreaming of a perfect family, full of love and at least four children. I decided that regardless of any circumstances, I would return Vito's love, and we would be happy together.

It was now one month before my wedding and almost everything was ready. We had mailed the invitations, reserved the church of Santa Rita, and had chosen a restaurant, the Sala delle Rose, for the reception. According to Italian customs, three weeks before the wedding I had an open house to allow family and friends to see all the things I had prepared. I was so proud of everything, because it had all been bought with my own money. From that day on, presents began to arrive from friends and relatives. I was still a little worried about the bridal veil, but finally Papa's brother, Rino, and his wife, Mona, gave me the money for the veil as a wedding present. The day before the wedding I purchased my veil.

Deep in my heart I always hoped that on my wedding day a miracle would happen. Bruno would appear somewhere and yell out, "Don't marry him!" I knew that if that had happened, I would have run away with him. I felt guilty and stupid about entertaining those thoughts, and decided to focus only on making my wedding day special. I knew I had a man who loved me dearly and I told myself to stop dreaming foolish things. My life would be perfect, and I would be happy at any cost. Our little home was now all in order waiting for us.

When the big day arrived. I got up at 6:00 a.m. more scared than ever. I had a big crunch in my stomach and was not feeling well, because I had not slept much. I had coffee with Mama, and we both got ready. I had to be in church at 6:30 for confession. I was supposed to have gone the day before, but with all the confusion I had forgotten. The weather was terrible. It was still dark and rainy. I hoped in my heart that it would become sunny. After confession, I spent a little time at the altar, praying and reflecting. I prayed with all my heart that God would give us his blessings and that we would be happy together.

Back at home, we woke everyone up, and I helped Mama get the house ready. The wedding would take place at 10:30 a.m. Romina and Mama helped me put on my wedding dress. Since it was wintertime, the dress was made of heavy brocade and had a very tight bodice. The skirt was floor length and a cape, attached at the shoulders, was longer than the dress and had a border of ostrich feathers which also continued around the sleeves.

The hairdresser came over and fixed my hair. It was a simple style, but I liked it right away. My veil had three white roses on the top and smaller little white flowers which came down around my face. The veil was thirty-eight feet long. Mama fixed my veil in place and Romina added the final touch, a little lipstick. The bride was ready.

Mama was very nervous, but looked beautiful in the dress I made her. It was green with a hand-embroidered bodice and an overcoat of black macramé. Papa wore a dark blue suit. When he saw me, he gave me a big hug and began to cry. My little nephew, Aldo, was the ring bearer and Beatrice, the daughter of a friend, was the flower girl. She was carrying a beautiful bouquet of white roses and orange tree blossoms that Vito had bought for me. My paternal grandparents looked more elegant than ever. Aurora and her family and all my other siblings were ready too.

The photographer arrived and behind him was the black Cadillac to take me to church. I was happy and when the time came to go to church, I looked around me and realized that my life as a young girl was almost over. I had become a woman. I was disappointed when I stepped outside. The sun was not shining brightly as I had hoped and it was still raining. A small crowd of bystanders had stopped to see the bride. I was shaking because it was cold and also because of my emotions, I clung tightly to Papa's arm. He reassured me with a bright smile and helped me get into the car.

At church I was helped by someone with an umbrella so I would not get wet. As soon as I stepped out of the car, I saw Vito standing by the church door waiting for me. He had a big smile on his face. When I approached him, he kissed my hand and gave me the bridal bouquet. Still at my father's arm, having cut the white ribbon tied on the doorway, I walked slowly toward the altar. The organ was playing Schubert's "Ave Maria." Tears started rolling down my face, and I began to shake. Was it truly me who was getting married?

At the altar Papa delivered me to Vito and the ceremony started. I cried throughout the entire ceremony. I could not stop. Vito noticed and asked: "What's wrong? Are you sorry?" I told him that I was not, but at the moment of saying my vows, a thought of Bruno crossed my mind. I told myself once again that I was crazy, that I had a good man who loved me, and I firmly responded, "Yes, I do." I looked toward the statue of Jesus, and I solemnly promised with all my heart that from that day on my life would be all for Vito. That I would love him with all my heart, be faithful to him, and try to be the best wife ever. And so I became Mrs. Vito Avella.

After the ceremony, Vito lifted my veil and kissed me on the forehead while going out of the church. Everyone was smiling and wishing us well. From the church we went to visit my grandma Anna who had a stroke a couple of years earlier, and with whom I had lived for a few years before the wedding. My cousin Romina and I took turns helping her around, especially at night if she needed to get out of bed. Grandpa had died the year before, and all the kids were now helping Grandma around. The little lady was very moved and happy to see me in my bridal attire. She hugged both of us and gave us an antique sterling silver tray as a gift. It was a gift to her, on her wedding day, from the Prince of Italy who resided in Palermo and was very attached to her family.

From Grandma's house we went to the factory where I worked. All the girls were waiting for us with a beautiful bouquet of fresh flowers. Mr. Poitano, the owner of the place, had been a best man at the wedding. From there we went to the Sanctuary of Santa Rosalia and then to the Royal Palace Gardens for the wedding pictures.

When we got to the reception hall, it was snowing. As we entered, the band was playing a song, "Oggi sposi," which means "Today We Marry." Between taking pictures and dancing, time went by very fast. I had hardly touched my food. By the time we were leaving the reception I felt sick. But we had to go home and quickly change our clothes, so we could take the cruise boat to Naples for our honeymoon. I whispered in Mama's ear that I needed her help and I asked if she could come with me to help me prepare. Mama looked at me with half a smile and said: "Daughter of mine, you don't have any need for me any longer." Vito came to hold my hand and we left.

At our new apartment Vito was very nervous, almost shaking. He lifted me up and placed me on our bed hugging me very gently. I was really scared, and I arose and locked myself in the bathroom, where I began to weep. After a while Mama and my mother-in-law arrived. When Vito told them what happened, they made me open the bathroom door. I clung to Mama, but she reassured me that it all would be all right. She helped me prepare and left. Vito was very disappointed, but soon got over it and was more kind than ever.

When we arrived at the port to leave for our honeymoon, I was wearing a beige and blue suit with a hat of the same color and brown shoes and bag. Vito looked at me with love and kissed me. He too looked nice. At the wedding he wore a dark gray suit but now he was now wearing a light gray one.

At the port, everybody was waiting for us and gave us red and white flowers. Among hugs and kisses, we boarded the ship. Again Papa gave me a big hug and told Vito to take good care of me. So our life together started. As the ship was leaving the harbor, I could still hear everybody's voice shouting my name. Vito was kind and attentive. He looked at me with loving eyes, as if I were a precious jewel. I truly wanted to love him too and I began to fall more in love with him.

The following morning when we arrived in Naples, we happily prepared to get off the ship, but we saw no one. We waited for a long time and finally an officer asked us if we were waiting for anyone. Vito answered that we were waiting to get off. The officer started to laugh and said that we were the only ones on the ship and we were trying to get out from the wrong side. We also laughed and made fun of ourselves. And for a long time we would laugh when recalling that incident. We spent three days in Naples touring the whole Amalfi coast. The weather had improved and it was quite sunny to suit our happy mood. In Naples we met a couple celebrating their fiftieth anniversary. I told Vito that I too wanted to go back to Naples to celebrate our fiftieth anniversary. Vito smiled. In Rome too, the weather was fine and the city was absolutely magnificent. We visited the Vatican City and Pope Paul VI, who gave us a rosary and a family book. We had the most fun in Rome, but soon it was time to go back home.

Vito began to work, and I began my duties as a wife and a homemaker. I was happy and forgot all the past events. My little apartment was lovely. It had two large rooms, a smaller room, a kitchen, and a small bathroom. It was on the second floor of a brand-new condominium and had two balconies, one of each side of the building. It was a very sunny place and I really loved it. Vito was madly in love with me and I cooked the best dishes for him and kept the house spotless. I looked forward to his coming home at night and waited for him with a smile on my face. Life was really good.

Three months after our wedding I discovered that I was

expecting our first child. What happiness! I would be a mother! Vito was also elated. The baby would be born in December, a winter baby. I soon began to feel sick and stopped eating. For the first four months, I had no strength at all and when I went to visit Mama, she practically spoon-fed me. At the end of the second trimester, my conditions improved and I began to prepare things for the baby. I started to feel such happiness, especially once the baby began to move inside of me. I bought a crib which I decorated with my bridal veil and kept my vigil. The waiting was wonderful even though I was still sick. My husband was so attentive. My sister Aurora was also pregnant and had her baby three months before I did. Finally she had a girl whom she named Susanna.

Two months before the delivery date, Vito began talking about going to America and he seemed very serious. I was opposed and tried to convince him otherwise. We were doing well, we had a nice home, and besides we were going to have a baby shortly after. A couple of days later he seemed to have forgotten about his idea.

On December 5, 1967, at one o'clock in the morning, our son was born. The delivery was at home in the presence of Mama, my mother-in-law, and naturally Vito and the doctor. The delivery went well and our happiness was complete when we discovered we had a son, just what we were hoping for. We named him Santino. What a perfectly beautiful baby. He was so tender and to hold him. Oh to hold him, what a gift! A true gift from God. Vito was so happy to be a daddy. We were truly happy. Santino was growing more beautiful everyday and his blue eyes were like two stars in the sky.

On January 13, 1968, a massive earthquake shook Sicily. Many little towns were destroyed, and Palermo, too, was severely damaged. I was so scared! We passed moments of sheer terror especially since the aftershocks continued for a few days after the earthquake. It was early in the morning, and I had just finished bathing Santino. All at once I heard a terrible noise and saw the walls of my apartment fold down. Full of terror, I grabbed the baby and moved in a corner of the house not knowing what to do next. Vito arrived a few minutes later, frantically looking for me and the baby. Thank God, we survived and so did many other people and thank God that earthquakes, even though terrible, are only fleeting moments.

When Santino was six months old, Vito's boss started talking about layoffs. Vito again started talking about migrating to the United States. I really did not like the idea, especially since he wanted to go alone. The fighting began. Vito would not listen to me. Encouraged by his parents, he started the paperwork and applied for a passport. He did not care about how I felt and kept telling me that he would leave all by himself, spend a year and look for a house for me and the baby. Furthermore, he decided that I would not live in our house, but move in with his parents.

The idea of leaving my house made me feel sick. I loved our little nest, but I was unable to convince him otherwise. I was so depressed that I got sick. My stomach was hurting so badly for a whole week, but I didn't even go to the doctor. It was the last couple of days that my husband would be with me and our son. I was so scared that I would never see him again.

On August 16, 1968, Vito left for the United States. Santino was eight months old and, when saying good-bye held Vito tightly as if he understood and was saying: "No, Papa, No Papa." I ,too, held him tightly, crying and feeling in my heart that my life would from then on would change for the worse. Vito had tears in his eyes, but was still firm and left. I was left at the airport watching the plane leave. I felt as if life itself was leaving me. I held Santino tightly, and forced myself back to the car. I had no strength left.

Chapter 4
From Happiness to Solitude

After Vito's departure a new life started for me. I moved in with my in-laws and everything was so different. I was raised in a family with loving parents, who were not ashamed to show it. To the contrary, my in-laws were cold and rigid. I felt uncomfortable around them.

I shared a bedroom with Vito's younger brother, Sarino, and two sisters, Ella and Giovanna. I really missed my husband and the privacy of our home. After two weeks, I started feeling really sick. I had stomach pains again and this time I had to go to the doctor. After the examinations I was told that I had gall bladder stones. I would have to have surgery to remove them and would have to stay in the hospital until I recovered.

A new mother, I was reluctant to leave the baby with Vito's parents, but I had no choice. My mother-in-law decided not to let my husband know about my stay in the hospital. She reasoned that her son "had to be happy to work!" I felt so lonely and had such desire to speak to my husband and hold my baby in my arms, but my mother-in-law kept telling me to relax that the baby was fine and did not even miss me. Her words hurt me and when my husband's letters arrived, I collected them and even took one with me to the surgery room. His loving words were of comfort to me.

The operation went well, and afterwards Mama comforted me, giving me strength and courage. We talked a lot, but I never told her that I was not happy living with my in-laws.

One day my in-laws brought Santino to visit me. What

pain I felt when I realized that Santino was reluctant to come to me. They laughed and said, "Don't you see, your son doesn't even need you?" I pulled Santino from my sister-in-law's arms and held him tightly. After awhile Santino seemed happy to be with me. I was at peace again.

I spent a month in the hospital and after my return my life became harder than ever. I just did not feel comfortable in my in-laws house. We did not communicate; they behaved differently, cooked differently, everything about them seemed to annoy me. Sometimes, whenever I could not stand it any longer, I would find an excuse to go to my little apartment. Once there I would cry my heart out. But that did not last for long either. Vito instructed his parents to rent a bigger house for all of us so we could be more comfortable. This meant my little apartment had to go. I was so upset and opposed to the idea, but could not do anything. They found a large house and they gave me two rooms so I could bring all my belongings and furniture. Although I did not have the privacy of my own home, at least I could have my own bedroom and could close the door behind me.

The months went by slowly. I was writing to my husband daily and he too wrote very frequently. His letters were full of love and devotion, but I still felt very lonely. All I had was my beautiful baby. And beautiful he really was, with his big blue eyes which enlightened his little round face surrounded by brown curls. He was very smart, and at six months he had already started saying, "Papa." At one year he could already verbalize many things. I remember that on his first birthday he began to walk and whenever I reprimanded him for something, he would look up at my big wedding picture on the wall and say: "Come down, Papa!" That was great amusement for me. My in-laws were very fond of Santino, but not of me.

I began to confide in Mama the few times I was able to visit her. Although we lived on the same street, I had to ask permission of my mother-in-law to go visit my own mother. I felt as if in a jail. Mama was very sad to see me in these conditions and she often asked me to spend the night at her house, but I had to refuse for fear of my in-laws. They claimed that their son had entrusted me to them and that I had to stay with them. If anyone came to visit me, they were not pleased. I wanted to leave, but whenever I left, it was always the same story. I had to ask permission and explain where I was going and when I expected to return. I was treated like a child. My only escape was to go visit Mama or Aurora, so Santino could play with my niece, Susanna.

One day I was allowed to visit Lidia, a girl I had met during my stay at the hospital. Of course, one of Vito's younger sisters went with me and spent the whole afternoon with us. Lidia had two very sweet little daughters, and was alone because her husband had left her. She lived with her parents and her mother was taking care of the girls. While in the hospital, she had no visitors at all. Lidia and I shared the same room and we had spent days talking to each other about our common miseries. She was really nice and Mama had grown fond of her too.

Lidia would often tell me of all her pains. She had married a good-for-nothing kind of man and she was paying for it. She had been hospitalized for appendicitis and I was helping her out. I comforted her, I got things for her, and at night I even tied the belt of my robe to her bed, so she could wake me up if she needed me. Whenever Mama brought me something, she also would think about Lidia who was so grateful she often cried of joy. When I was operated on, Lidia returned all my favors, helping and assisting me in any way possible. We became very close, like two sisters. She actually called Mama, "Mama" and my father, "Papa." Such a dear, sweet girl. Lidia was happy to see me again. Her mother received me warmly, and time flew very quickly.

When my sister-in-law and I left Lidia's house, it was later than expected. My father-in-law was really upset and said, "That's the last time you visit that good for nothing woman!" He then hit his daughter for not keeping track of the time. I felt so sorry for my sister-in-law! I ran into my room with Santino. Hurt, I refused to come out for supper.

My father-in-law was a real authoritarian. Small in stature and of dark features, he could still impose his presence on all of us. He had a scar that went from his left eye to his neck and always made him look mad, which really scared me.

A few days later I told Mama what had happened and this time she became really mad. The following day she decided to talk to my in-laws. They had the usual story. They were responsible for my behavior, and there was no way Mama could convince them otherwise. I felt as if I were under house arrest. I could not bear it any longer, yet, when I wrote to Vito, I never told him anything. I would beg him to expedite the proceeding for my departure, so I could join him in the States.

I started preparing my document for the departure, and when my passport was ready, I went to the American consulate to get the visa. The consul told me that I could not have a visa because he had already given one to my husband. He added that my husband had to come into the office and applied for my visa. My heart came to a full stop. My legs were shaking, and I could hardly get out of that office. I began to understand the whole thing! They all knew that I could not join my husband without his consent! How stupid I had been! I felt cheated. I began to resent my in-laws, and husband as well. I was sure, that he also knew that I could go nowhere without him. When I wrote him a letter explaining the situation, he claimed that he knew nothing about it.

The months went slowly by and spring arrived with its sunny days and wonderful flowers that I so loved. Strangely though, I was totally apathetic, had lost all strength, and was losing weight almost daily. I hoped so much that Vito would come back. I would often think about our little nest, full of love and how happy we had been there. It seemed like an eternity had gone by. Santino was growing strong and healthy. He was my only joy, but how sad that Vito could not hear all the words our baby was learning.

Angelo decided to get married in July and I volunteered to sew clothes for the whole family. It was the perfect opportunity to go to my Aunt's Lia's house, the one who made my wedding dress. My aunt was indeed a very good dress designer, and so I was helping her, as she directed my work. At that time I was still a bit scared to actually design clothes myself. I was not in any hurry, so I would go in the morning and stay at her house until evening. Her husband Matteo was Mama's brother, and he too, like Uncle Giacomo, was a very cheery person. He always tried to make me laugh. Since he was a retiree, he would watch Santino and play with him while my aunt and I worked on the dresses. At night, I would go back into my prison.

The weeks went by and I felt so strangely. I was not hungry and did not have an appetite. I kept on losing weight, and I felt like I had no strength at all. Mama would come to visit some nights and bring me a steak sandwich which she forced me to eat alone in my room. She thought that I was not eating because I did not like my mother-in-law's cooking. But I had gotten used to her cooking and even liked it at some point.

One morning as I was preparing to go to work at Aunt Lia's house, as usual, I had no energy at all. I was tempted to stay in bed, but I wanted to leave that house. So I got ready, put the baby in the carriage, and set out for my aunt's house. My God, the carriage was so heavy! What was happening to me? My legs were shaking. In order to go to my aunt's house, I had to walk in front of my parents' house, and when I arrived to the house next door to theirs, Aunt Melina, my father's sister, was looking out of the window. She noticed that I was having a hard time pushing the carriage. As soon as I got near her window, I stopped to say hello, but before I could greet her she asked: "What's wrong with you today?" I said I was fine, but she continued: "Have you looked at yourself in the mirror? Your eyes are yellow, and you look dead!" I insisted that I was fine, and that it was just her impression. But at the same time my sister Aurora arrived with her children and as soon as she saw me, she became alarmed. She made me get inside and said she was calling the doctor. I kept insisting that I was fine, but they didn't listen. Mama took care of the children, and Aurora took me to the doctor who was also her brother-in-law and who had known me for a long time.

Dr. Randazzo took one look at me and asked my sister: "And how is it that you just noticed that she is really sick?" His diagnosis was that I had a very advanced case of viral hepatitis and needed to be hospitalized immediately. I cried my heart out. I did not want to go to the hospital again and leave my baby! Dr. Randazzo took pity on me and said that he would take care of me at home as long as I listened to him and followed all his directions. He did all the blood work in his lab and sent me home giving my sister the instructions to follow. I had to stay in bed for a good while. My thoughts went astray. Would I be well again? Would I ever be able to see my husband again? Sensing that I was troubled, Aurora reassured me that all would be well.

My hepatitis was very serious. Every hour I was turning more and more yellow. When I got home, Mama put me to bed and told me that I would stay at her house and that she would take care of me. In the meantime, she had sent Lisa to get my mother-in-law. When my mother-in-law arrived, she yelled at Mama, because they had taken me to the doctor without her consent. Mama tried to explain what had happened, but she was offended. Finally she said to Mama, "Well, you take care of your daughter, but I will take Santino

with me, because I don't want the baby to get infected too."
Mama was very firm and said no. She knew that I would die
if Santino went back to that house. Finally, my mother-in-law
left, very upset and infuriated.

My mother-in-law was overweight, with very short brown
hair, a round face, a tiny nose, and small, dark eyes. She
never had anything nice to say to me and always had to have
the last word. I did not argue with her, although she was
usually harsh with me. I had once been fond of her, and I
even respected her until I was forced to live with her. I
thanked God for Mama.

My illness was a long one. I spent days cared for and
spoiled by my Mama who worked so hard juggling taking
care of me and Santino. She was also helping my brother
with the wedding preparations. Mama was really busy but
never complained at all. At night, Papa would sit with me,
and we would talk for hours. All day there was somebody
close to me: they never left me alone for one minute. My
cousin Romina who had married her blue-eyed man before
my illness, came to visit me almost daily. They all took
Santino to the playground, and I was not in need of anything. I had to stay in bed and had lost so much weight that
I was a skeleton. The medications were expensive, and I
depleted the little savings that I had.

Vito knew nothing about of what had happened, since his
parents had decided that he should not know. He wrote regularly, and every month he sent me a check to pay his parents
for rent and food. From that money I was able to put a little
aside, but after paying doctor bills and medicine, I had nothing left. My brothers picked up some of the bills. My mother-
in-law seldom came to visit, and only once she brought me a
fruit basket. Even Rosetta, who was my best friend, seldom
showed up and when she did, she was very cold towards me.

A month after my illness, my brother got married. My
aunt finished making all the clothes that I had started and

even made a dress for me. Mama and Papa helped me get out of bed even though I could hardly stand up. During the wedding they took care of the baby, and I just sat through the whole wedding. The ceremony was a beautiful. It was July, and it was hot, but not too much. The sky was a brilliant blue and shining in all its splendor. The bride and groom were happy as ever. My brother was very elegant, and Tina had the most elegant and expensive dress made of hand-embroidered organza. Everything went well, and I was so happy for them. However, I was looking forward to getting back in bed. I was really tired and exhausted, but I tried to smile so that Mama would be happy too.

Vito was writing very often, but his letters were no longer full of loving words as in the beginning. I could feel a change in him, and I blamed myself. Perhaps I should have insisted more and not allowed him to go. We should not have separated for so long. I wondered and wondered without reaching any answers. I was depressed, still sick, and bedridden.

One day, Mama had to go out and I was left alone at home. She told me not get up for any reasons at all. She said she would be gone for about half an hour and was taking Santino with her. About five minutes after she left, someone knocked at the door. I did not want to get up, but then I thought to myself, who knows, it could be Vito! I rose to get out of bed with my heart beating very fast.

My legs were shaking, as I tried to rush to the door fearing that he would go away. I got to the door and tried to open it and then everything went dark. I woke back up on the bed, and there was a lot of confusion around me. I opened my eyes to see Mama all worried. Tina, her sister, my aunt, and even Santino were all staring at me looking very worried. Then I remembered what had happened. My sister-in-law, Tina, said that she had seen the door handle turn, but the door had not opened. She had called several times, and when no one answered, she and her sister pushed the door open and found me laying on the floor. I had passed out, and they had carried me back to bed and tried to revive me.

Two months had gone by since the onset of my illness, and my hepatitis was still serious. One morning, while Mama was changing my bed, I looked at myself on the mirror. Was it possible that I was so skinny? Never in my life I had looked worse. Why was my healing process so slow? In my heart I did not want to get well. And yet, everybody was so dear to me! Papa had even allowed me to sleep in his bed, next to Mama, and had spent so many hours with me. He wanted to know everything, what I wanted in life, what I wanted to eat. He wanted to see me happy, but I knew that he was really worried for me.

Oh, how sweet my Papa was! Santino also was crazy about his grandpa, who would spoil him and take him for long walks. Santino would always call Papa, "Nonno Aldo!" and wait all day long until grandpa came home from work.

One morning the telephone rang. Mama answered it and looked stunned. It was Vito calling for the very first time! Holding on to Papa's arm, I made it to the phone with my heart in my throat. He asked me how I was doing and told me that he was coming to Palermo in two weeks. I was so happy, I hugged Papa and yelled out for joy. Vito was coming! I felt crazy for the joy! They immediately put me back in bed, and I relaxed a little. I felt like my life was returning back inside of me. From that moment I began to smile and eat and especially, I began to improve. A couple of days later the doctor came for his usual visit, and he was really impressed by my improvement. He was happy for me. He told me I could now get out of bed, and took me off some medications. Everyone was happy for my progress. The blood analysis came back negative. Thank God! To celebrate Mama bought some fabric of white cotton so my aunt could make me a pretty dress. They were all so close to me physically and mentally!

Two days before Vito's arrival, my brother Stefano confessed that he had written to Vito and told him about my condition. In fact, he had asked him to come before it was too late. I was scared that my in-laws would find out. Anyway, I did not think about it and decided to focus on Vito's arrival. That same day I found out that my uncle too had written to Vito, as Stefano had. That's why Vito was coming back to Palermo. The day before the arrival, my mother-in-law and Rosetta came to visit me and brought some medicines suggested by their doctor. They recommended that I take them, and I said I would, but threw them out as soon as they left.

The big day finally arrived. Vito was traveling with the *Michelangelo* ship and had been at sea for seven days. I had counted each of those days. A year had passed by since we last saw each other and so much had happened. But I believed everything would return to the way it was before.

Feeling fine, I dressed and went down to the port with my whole family. We arrived just in time to see the ship come into the harbor. Vito had told me that he would fly a red little flag so I would see him in the crowd on the deck.

Everyone on the port was trying to recognize someone. I finally saw Vito's red flag. The ship was enormous, and people looked so tiny, but when the ship came to a full stop, I could see him clearly. He blew me a kiss and waved his hands. It was such a joy! Vito got off the ship and ran toward me. He hugged me and took the baby in his arms. Everybody who came to the port was pulling on him anxious to greet him.

My happiness suddenly fled when I noticed that he kept looking toward the ship. There was a young woman waving at him. I asked him who she was and he said: "When you travel on a ship for so long, you make a lot of friends." I forgot about the girl, but when we got to his parents' house, I heard him telling his mother about the wonderful cruise and the beautiful girl he had met. Her name was Manuela, and she was from Brazil, very nice, very rich and traveling to Italy alone. He had a wonderful time with her. I was totally devastated. Was it possible? Was that Vito speaking? I calmed myself down and told myself that it was no big deal, and that I should not allow his comments about Manuela ruin our beautiful day.

When everybody left and we went to our room, Vito was very thoughtful but cold. After a year he seemed to have no desire to hold me in his arms. He did not tell me that he loved me, nor that he had missed me. Instead in an icy cold voice, he said, "You don't look like you are sick. Your brother told me you were about to die. Did you trick me into coming back?" "Indeed I have been very sick, but I improved especially since I heard that you were coming." I said.

Vito did not answer, but I was so hurt. Did he really think that way? Was he unhappy that I was no longer sick? I realized his feeling for me had changed and felt a pain in my heart. The following days he seemed happier to be back, and I did my best to show him how much I loved him, while Santino followed him around like a little puppy.

Vito had been able to save some money, and we started looking for a house to buy, but we soon realized that we did not have enough money. A month after his return, Vito was already tired of living in Palermo and wanted to return to the United States. He said he needed at least two years to make more money. This time I tried to stop him with all my strength. I sternly told him, "Either we all leave, or you stay!" I refused to go back to the life I had before. I had not dreamed of such a marriage.

Vito agreed, but we had the problem of my visa. Then a travel agency in Palermo suggested that we try to go to the States through Canada. It was risky, and Vito tried to convince me to let him go alone. His other excuse was that he did not have a place for all of us. Thank God Vito's uncle decided to help us, so we started all the paperwork to leave together.

I was happy that I would go with him, but my heart was full of sadness. I had to leave my whole family. And what if I would never see them again? I had not left them for twenty-three years, and I was leaving for such a faraway land! I tried not to think. Mama was encouraging me, but I knew she was sad too, and whenever she looked at me, her eyes were full of tears. All my siblings were sad. I went to visit Luigi in jail. He was sad and also feeling guilty about what he had done to me. I hugged him and told him that I had forgiven and forgotten. The day of the departure arrived very quickly.

Chapter 5
Good-bye to My Sicily

November 2, 1969, the day of the departure, was a sunny, beautiful day. I could smell the scent of the orange blossoms and of the jasmine in the air even though those flowers were out of season. I looked at everything carefully as to impress on my memory all the shapes and colors of my homeland. I knew I would never find another place as beautiful as my Palermo, and that I never would be able to forget my hometown.

Before leaving, I wanted to revisit all the places dear to me: Monte Pellegrino, the Ultiveggio Castle, Mondello, La Favorita, and especially, the convent of San Giuseppe, where I spent a couple of hours with Sister Maria. Finally, I prayed at the chapel of the convent. Sister Maria encouraged me with these words: "Anna, remember that marriage is just like any vocation, and your mission has just started." We hugged and promised to write to each other.

All my things and furniture were left at Vito's parents' house. We only took our personal belongings, two suitcases in all. Vito was very excited, but I was sad about leaving. Not because I did not want to go with him, but because leaving my family was really harder than I had thought. I remembered my childhood, the happy and the sad times, but especially the love which reigned in my family, and I cried. But I had to go. My place was with my husband and son, and from that day it was truly a new life.

On the way to the airport, I could see the beauty of the sea and hear the waves breaking on the cliffs. The little island of Femmina was far away and looked lonely and sad;

on the opposite side the mountains, green and blue, tall and majestic. I was looking at everything carefully to make them mine forever, a permanent part of my mind and my heart. The airport was at the foothill of the mountain range, right between the mountains and the sea. Between cries and hugs, I separated from everybody and while climbing on the plane and waving, the last face I saw was Papa's. After takeoff, I could see my whole city, beautiful and mysterious, with all the countryside full of orange, tangerine and lemon trees. I could see for a couple of more minutes and then, it was all gone. My throat was tight while I was saying good-bye to my land. Throughout the flight, Vito was holding my hand, and Santino was cuddling me.

The plane landed in New York and we got off, but we could not exit the airport. The immigration authorities directed us to the connecting flight to Canada. We had decided that from Canada we would smuggle ourselves back to New York. So we boarded the plane for Toronto and there, after regulating our visas, we took a taxi to a hotel. We were exhausted, and Santino was restless. At the hotel Vito made some phone calls, talked to a few people, and finally we were able to sleep.

The following morning there was a man waiting for us in the hotel lounge. He only said, "Mr. and Mrs. Avella?" We nodded, and he asked us to follow him. He put us on a bus and told us which stop to get off and whom we would meet. When we did get to the designated bus stop, nobody was there. We waited for a short while and then when the crowd dwindled, a man approached us and again asked us if we were the Avellas. We walked over to his car and got in. After driving for a couple of miles, the driver stopped to renegoti-ate the deal with Vito. He wanted more money than origi-nally agreed, because he had not been told that there was also a baby. My husband said he would only pay when we arrived at his uncle's house in Queens, New York.

Our trip to New York, no, our adventure, started. We traveled the whole night on dark back roads. I was very scared and held on to Vito and the baby. Santino cried all night long, he was tired and hungry. We could not stop anywhere, and besides there were no stores in sight.

At dawn we arrived in New York. My husband paid the man and I thanked God that all went well. Vito's uncle and aunt were waiting for us, and so was my father-in-law, who had arrived there about a month before. Vito's aunt said that she only had room for me and the baby. I was alarmed because I did not know or trust these people. I did not want to separate from my husband. But, Vito insisted that it was the only way and that he would soon find a house and we would move together.

The day after our arrival, I was left alone while everybody went to work. Vito lived in Brooklyn, New York, with his father and three cousins and came to visit me about once a week. I was sorry about being separated from Vito again, and living with people I did not know. A month later, Vito finally rented an apartment and bought a bedroom set, a little bed for Santino, and a table with four chairs. When he came to get me and it made my whole day. I thanked his relatives for their hospitality and left with him.

During the taxi ride to Brooklyn, I was able to see the man-made wonders-bridges, skyscrapers, trains that ran above and under the ground. Everything looked so strange. It was beautiful, but not for me. I was longing for the scenic sights of my homeland. I told myself to get used to it, since this was going to be home. When we arrived at the apartment and saw its unsanitary condition I began to cry. I had never seen anything dirtier or uglier! My first reaction was to start cleaning. Vito had already started his job as a night baker and went to work that same night. So I spent my first night alone, with Santino. I was terrorized and depressed, but I tried to be strong. I kept repeating to myself "get used to it."

The following day my father-in-law moved in with us. I was happy just to have another soul to speak to when Vito was working. He worked at a Brooklyn restaurant. I cooked for him, looked after him, and tried to be as kind as possible. He was very fond of Santino and not bad company at all, except for his authoritative ways. But then, he also suffered asthma attacks, and I felt sorry for him.

Our two-bedroom apartment was old, but had many windows. The sunlight shining through the windows made it so cheery. From one large window I could see the Brooklyn Bridge. The street had no trees, but was busy with a lot of traffic. We lived on the second floor of a four-family complex. Vito worked at night and slept during the day. He did not want to be bothered at all, not even to go grocery shopping. Whenever he had free time, he would usually go out with his friends and return home the next day, which led to arguments.

A new life had started, but it was life of bitterness and solitude. I tried to be a perfect wife, even when he would bring his friends to the house for a night of gambling and drinking. But I began to notice that Vito was drinking heavy alcohol.

Next to our apartment lived another Sicilian family to whom I had grown attached. I was especially fond of Grazia, a very dear lady who had two little children, Luciano and Mariella. The little one, Mariella was a year older that Santino who was now two. The kids played very well together.

The solitude was becoming unbearable. Vito had grown detached from me. Some days he was affectionate, but for the most part, he ignored me rarely taking me or Santino out. I felt completely isolated in the apartment.

Three months went by, and I discovered I was pregnant again. Vito and I were happy, but I felt scared too. Lorena, a lady who worked with Vito, offered to take me to the doctor for the first time and then she did for the following nine months. It was a difficult pregnancy, and I was really sick. In the meantime my father-in-law had returned to Italy. I had less work to do, but I still felt lonely.

Vito was wrapped in his new life. In the last month of my pregnancy, the next-door neighbor stayed close to me. When Vito went out, she would stay with me until he returned. Vito did not give me the phone number of his job. I hoped I would not need anything when he was away from home.

One night, Vito went out with his friends and did not return home until 7:00 a.m. the following day. I had been frantically waiting all night. When he walked in, I began yelling in a hysterical fit of rage. Vito flung himself against me and started hitting me. I cried for help, but he continued to hit me. Little Santino did not understand what was going on, but he cried when as he watched his papa hit me.

The next day Grazia, my neighbor, told me she heard everything and was really sorry. I did not speak to him for a few days. I cried hard and blamed myself.

When I began labor, thank God Vito was at home and took me to the hospital. Grazia offered to keep Santino. I was very grateful to her and sure that she was a great mother and fond of Santino. Lorena came to the hospital with me and accompanied me all the way to the delivery room. Vito dropped me off and left.

My delivery was a horrible experience. The nurses spoke to me in English. I could not understand a word. The labor pains increased, and I tried to stay calm. Oh God, how I wished Mama were there with her reassuring smile. I was so lonely, and I prayed really hard until the doctor came and delivered me of a beautiful nine-pound baby boy. It was November 23, 1970.

Vito came to the hospital and looked happy, but only stayed a little while. When I saw my baby, I was speechless. I forgot all my problems. Fabio was so perfect! He had the cutest round face and a tiny nose. His complexion was milky white and he was admired by the staff.

Since my delivery was difficult, I could not get up from bed. Whenever I tried, blood would run down my legs. I was so lonely especially seeing other women surrounded by their husbands and family members. And all their flowers. I had nobody. Vito came everyday but only for about five minutes. Whenever I called him on the phone, he never answered.

I was released from the hospital after five days. Santino greeted me with a sad face. He was a little jealous of the little baby in my arms. Right away, I gave Fabio to Grazia so I could spend time with Santino. He hugged and kissed me and was then ready to see his little brother.

From that moment on, I could not rest. Grazia would take care of Santino and leave her front door open. If I needed anything, I could just yell across the hall. I was not feeling well, but did not want to totally depend on my friend. I tried to do things around the house, but often had to stop because of stomach and back pains. Vito was not helping me much with the housework, nor taking me grocery shopping. I had to do all the washing by hand, and at night I would go to bed exhausted. I tried to be loving to my husband but sometimes, I lost my patience. When I did, Vito would hit me. When I pulled myself together, I would always convince myself that it was my fault Vito hit me and try not to think about it.

I never wrote to my parents about Vito's behavior, because it would just upset them. I would ask myself over and over what could be the causes of his personality change. I wondered but had no answers.

Fabio was growing healthy and strong; he was a good and sweet baby. Santino was affectionate and vivacious. He would never stay still, and finally, one day I convinced Vito to take Santino out. When they were out together, Vito asked his son not to call him "dad" in front of his friends, but to call him "uncle," and he told Santino not to tell me. But

Santino did tell me and it broke my heart. I did not say anything to Vito for fear that he would hit Santino. All these little things contributed to my feelings of loneliness. I missed my loving family all the more.

Back in Palermo, my brother Stefano had married Ninetta, and I was very sad to have missed their wedding. Lisa also had a boyfriend, and Rino had been drafted by the Italian Army. Angelo and his wife had their first child. They named him Aldo, after Papa. Luigi had finished his time in jail, and now he also had a girlfriend. Life was going on peacefully in Palermo, but life for me was filled with sadness and solitude. I decided to work at home. Vito kept telling me that we would only stay in America for three years before moving back home. I decided that by working I could help save some money.

The first dresses I made I sewed by hand, since I did not have a sewing machine. But with my first earnings I was able to buy one. I was therefore busy with sewing, the children, and the house. Then, my in-laws decided to move back to the States and bring their two youngest children Giovanna and Sarino. Their other daughter, Ella, had by now married. So we prepared one bedroom for the parents, while their kids would take Santino's room. Santino and Fabio would sleep in our bedroom. Vito was very happy. I was too, hoping that my mother-in-law had changed a little and would be good company for me. I even thought that my in-laws would straighten Vito's bad behavior, and I hoped to make them my allies.

Chapter 6
Lost Hopes

The family had suddenly grown, and the house was just too small. The first few days after my in-laws arrival, there was such a stream of visiting relatives that Vito did not go out at all. For a whole week, he stayed at home and gave me hopes that things were changing. It did not last long. Vito began to go out as usual. One morning my girlfriend, Grazia, told Vito's parents how badly Vito had treated me, especially during my pregnancy and asked them to help me. Upset, my mother-in-law answered, "My son is still young and must rightfully have some fun." Grazia and her husband could not believe their ears. How could a mother say such things?

Vito continued his partying and his parents did not seem to mind. Every evening, after I put the children to bed, I would sew late into the night. My mother-in-law would ask, "So, you came to America just to make another baby?" I suffered in silence. My sister-in-law Giovanna had made some friends, Rosa and Agata. Both girls were still teenagers, but they looked much older. Rosa was big and tall with dark eyes and brown hair. She was not very pretty. However, Agata was very beautiful. Rosa and Agata would come over sometimes to socialize. I was happy because I liked them. I was only twenty-five and needed young people around too. I felt so old!

Soon after I met Rosa and Agata, I began to notice that Vito was going out much less. Oh how that pleased me! Perhaps he was finally changing! "Oh my God, that would make me so happy!" Vito would sometimes ask me to go out with him, but his mother refused to watch the kids, so I had to decline his invitations.

Summer 1971 arrived with its unbearable heat. Our apartment did not have air conditioning, which made it suffocating and hot. My in-laws and their children got in the habit of going to a nearby park for a walk. Sometimes Vito would go with them. A couple of times, he asked me to join them, but I did not go because I had so much to sew. Eventually he gave up.

Going to the park did not matter to me until I noticed that whenever Agata came to the house, Vito would act differently. He didn't want to go out and he constantly stared at her. I tried to pay close attention to it. Was it possible that my husband would flirt right in my own home? I could not believe it, but the doubt was already in my mind, and I decided to explore the possibility.

One night I told my husband I too wanted to go to the park and he said, "What about your sewing?" "I am finished for the day," I replied. So we all walked to the park together. I pretended to watch the children, but I was watching Vito and Agata. Agata was sitting on a swing, laughing and giggling, and Vito was pushing her and whispering in her ears. In front of me, they would only speak English. Although I could not understand English, I understood that my husband was flirting with Agata.

One afternoon Vito left the house, and I decided to follow him. I saw him walking towards the park. When he started walking faster, I lost sight of him. Frantic I started crying and looking around for him, but I could not find him. I must have fallen down, because I came back home dirty with bleeding knees. After a couple of hours, Vito came back, all happy. Still crying, I told him I suspected that he was cheating on me. He told me I was a crazed woman and pushed me to the floor. He began to kick me and step on me. My nose began to bleed, but he did not seem to care. I was lying on the floor bruised and crying, as he left the house.

His mother never asked me anything, although she saw the black-and-blue marks all over my arms, face, and legs. I thought it was strange that she did not say anything to me about it. Didn't she even hear the children screaming? I could not look at myself in the mirror for days. I had two black eyes and a broken lip. My nose was swollen, and I looked totally disgusting. When I told her what I suspected, she said it was just the fruit of my imagination and my jealousy. For the first time since my marriage, my thoughts went to Bruno. "Oh Bruno, are you at least happy?"

The following night, after I put the children to bed, Vito approached me. But not to apologize, he wanted to have sex. "Do not touch me!," I screamed, rejecting him. But he insisted. Grabbing me by my hair, he pushed me to the floor. I continued to reject him, and he started hitting me again. I cried, as I tried to defend myself with all my strength, but he won. That episode left me totally shaken and feeling disgusted. I did not tell anyone, not even Grazia. I did not understand that I had been raped.

As the weeks went by my disgust turned to anger and resentment. Vito never said that he was sorry. Looking for someone to blame, I thought maybe it was my fault because I had rejected him. Or perhaps it was his parents fault. They should have taught him better.

Sometimes I would hear Vito talk to his friends about his childhood. He told them that when he was younger he could never go out, because any money he made he had to give to his father who was sick and did not work. He said he had to support his whole family. Now that he finally had a little money, he wanted to relive what he felt he had missed out on while growing up. He wanted to have fun. In America he had found not only money, but freedom.

Vito had worked since the age of eight. At ten, he came to Palermo to work, while his family lived in the nearby town of Bagheria. He worked in a deli and also slept there. During the day he went to school. I think his problems stemmed from his childhood. Despite how he treated me and the children, I believed Vito had a good heart and I continued to hope he would change.

When Fabio was a year old I began to work at a clothing factory, called Ciccio. My mother-in-law watched the children, and I paid her twenty-five dollars a week. I was not too happy to work outside of the house and leave the kids with her, but I needed the money. I thought that between what I earned at home and the factory job, we could put aside enough money to return to Italy.

It was worth the sacrifice, although leaving the children every morning was painful. Every night I looked forward to coming back home. I remember seeing Santino's sad face, as he stared out the window while waiting for me. As soon as I walked up the stairs, he would run to me and hug and kiss me. Even little Fabio would come and meet me wanting to be lifted up into my arms.

Fabio had started walking at ten months and was a very calm and sweet little boy. Vito's parents would fill my head with all the problems that Santino had caused during the day, and that would make me nervous. I felt like kicking the whole family out of my house, but I had to stay calm and be patient.

After two months, I found a better job, closer to home and with a higher salary. I could walk there, and I liked the bosses, two brothers in their sixties. On the first day, I came back home enthusiastic and began telling Vito and my in-laws all about my job and how much my bosses liked my work. All of a sudden, my father-in-law said, "Be careful where you step and how you behave. If you make any mistakes, I will not let you ruin my son, but I will kill you with my own hands. I will get a dull knife to hurt you more, and I will stick it down your throat."

I was speechless. A ice cold feeling swept down my spine. My husband started to laugh and said, "I have a better solution. I will put gasoline on you, and I will torch you." They all spoke so calmly as if it was everyday chit chat. I thought to myself, "They are either all crazy, or I am going completely insane!" I found the courage to ask my husband, "Is that what I should do with you?" Before he could answer me, his mother said, "You are a woman and must know your place! Your husband is a man, and men are hunters and hunt where they damn please."

I went to bed terrified. What was I doing wrong? Why did they all despise me? I wished so badly to have somebody near me who would love me. I could not continue this way. What a mistake it been to come to America, and I now was suffering the consequences. Oh, if only Mama knew what had happened to me and how unhappy I was! I had nobody to talk to or to confide in.

Back in Palermo, my brother Rino had gotten engaged, and so had Luigi. The only one at home was Lisa, who was also was already engaged to a boy named Diego, who was a baker. I kept in touch with Sister Maria, but never told her anything. I only asked that she should pray for me. Aurora knew a little about my situation, but I begged her not to tell the others and not to mention anything in her letters, because Vito read my mail.

Vito's sister, Giovanna, had gotten engaged to a man she had met at a wedding. Since her parents were going back to Sicily, she decided to have her wedding before their departure. I was happy that they were leaving. I could finally have some privacy, and, besides, they had done nothing at all to improve my lot.

One Saturday morning, Santino locked himself in the bathroom. I tried to explain to him what to do, but was so scared that he just cried, screamed, and kicked at the door. Vito was sleeping, but woke up when he heard Santino crying. As soon as Santino walked out of the bathroom, Vito grabbed him in a fit of rage and hit him.

I pulled Santino from his father's hands and noticed he

was bleeding from his nose and mouth. I screamed to the top of my lungs until Vito left. Then I pulled Santino to my heart and hugged him, reassuring him that I loved him. Still sobbing, Santino told me that his grandma and uncles beat him too. How could I have not noticed sooner? As I looked up I noticed Fabio standing in his crib crying too. I really knew how it felt to be hit, and I cried with them. I decided I would only work for two more months.

That night I had an incredible dream. I heard a child's cry coming out of the kitchen, and when I went there, Jesus was sitting at the table, with Fabio in his lap and Santino next to him. He had one hand on Santino's shoulder, and said, "These are my children. You must not touch them. Nobody must touch them." I stood quietly with my head lowered as if to say yes, and when he finished speaking, I tried to move. Then I woke up. I ran to the kitchen, but no one was there. Still shaking I went to the children's bedrooms and found them sleeping peacefully. I was scared and tried to analyze my dream. I thought, perhaps Jesus wanted to claim my children. Then I realized Jesus was telling me to put a stop to my children's abuse. I decided that nobody would ever lay a hand on my babies again!

Time went by slowly. Vito was working every night, and when he came back home, I went to work. When I came home, he was seldom there. One day, he told me that he had found another job in a pizzeria. He would work there on Saturday, his day off. "Working seven days a week is not a good idea," I said. But he insisted that we needed the money to go back home. So he now went to work on Saturdays too. One more year, and then I would be with my family in Sicily.

One Saturday, my in-laws, my brother-in-law and Rosa's friend, Marisa, decided to go to the theater to see a group of Italian singers. Vito went to work, and I stayed home with the children, as usual. After I put the children to bed I started to have suspicions. I tried to reject the ideas, but I could not.

It was as if an alarm went off in my heart. I tried to find the phone number of the pizzeria Vito was working at, which of course he had never given to me. I called the pizzeria and to my surprise I discovered that Vito had never worked in that place! And silly me, feeling sorry about his working seven days a week. I was so mad!

That night, he came home at 2:00 a.m. I did not want to open the door, but he started hitting and kicking the door until I finally opened. As soon as he walked in, we argued and he slapped me before finally walking out. Exhausted, I went back to bed. Around 3:00 a.m., I heard the rest of the family come in. I could hear the conversation through the paper thin walls, and my suspicion was confirmed. My husband had gone to the theater with them all, and in the sweet company of a new girlfriend.

Giovanna, my sister-in-law, was arguing with her mother. "What Vito is doing is really cruel. He has no right to date other girls," she said. Then I heard my mother-in-law say, "And are you so stupid that you will go and tell her tomorrow?" I wanted to break the wall down and tell them all I had already heard everything.

How could my mother-in-law continually defend Vito. Feeling hopeless, I just went back to bed.

While helping Giovanna prepare for her wedding, I discovered that I was pregnant again. It was the end of 1972. I was not happy at all; I did not want another child to experience the misery I lived in. Besides, my pregnancies had been difficult and I suffered a lot. So I quit my job and started sewing from home again.

Giovanna got married on January 31, 1973. I had been very busy helping her and had come to the decision that I would do anything possible to save my six-year-old marriage. As I worked on her wedding attire, I remembered how happy I had been in our first little home and how my happiness had vanished when I was forced to leave. I tried to talk to Vito, asking him if he found anything wrong with me. His insulting answer was that I was crazy.

Shortly after the wedding, my in-laws went back to Sicily, and I finally had some privacy again. After two years of having people always around the house, I looked forward to the future. We would soon go back too, and things would change for the better. At least those were my hopes.

After my in-laws left, Rosa, Giovanna's friend, started to visit quite often. Sometimes she came alone and sometimes with her mother. Rosa had been a bridesmaid at Giovanna's wedding, and so we had seen a lot of her. We became very close friends. Her mother was also very attached to me. Rosa was about seven years younger than me. She worked in a department store in Brooklyn and was engaged to a young, Italian man, who lived in Montelepre, a little town in the province of Palermo. They planned to marry in the fall.

Vito kept telling me that it would be better if I went back to Sicily before the baby's birth, so I would have Mama with me. He would join me in July or August. I said no at first, but then I agreed. He told me not to worry because we had enough money saved that we could settle permanently in Sicily.

During the following months, I was busy preparing for my departure. Rosa had asked Vito to be the best man at the wedding and she asked me to be the matron of honor. Since she was getting married in Montelepre, she knew we would already be in Palermo for the wedding.

My husband was behaving strangely, but I found nothing new it. Perhaps, I was really going crazy! I quit thinking about it and threw myself into my work. Vito went out every night, as usual, and Rosa and her mother kept me company. Santino was going to preschool and was really vivacious. He was very sharp, and his blue eyes were always looking for something to analyze. Fabio, as always, was sweet and calm. He spent most of the day attached to my skirt. I could not move without him always following me. He was happy baby and rarely cried—a true joy.

My parents wrote to me that they were very happy about our return. In the meantime another sad event had broken Mama's heart. Luigi had been caught stealing again, and was thrown in jail again. This time he left behind a pregnant wife, Maria. Mama was truly heartbroken, and Papa had to work hard again to pay lawyers' fees, and to take care of his pregnant daughter-in-law. It was really a hard life for Papa and Mama.

On Valentine's Day, Vito bought me a big heart-shaped box of chocolates. I was so surprised! He had never given me anything for Valentine's Day. Later that day, as we were getting ready to go to the doctor's office, he started the car but then remembered he had forgotten something in the house. He left me in the car and went back inside. On intuition, I decided to follow him. I walked upstairs and I waited behind the door, just in time to hear him sweetly talking on the phone and saying, "I'll see you tonight, honey." I pushed the door open and shouted, "I heard everything! You can not deny your unfaithfulness any longer." Angry that I had followed him, he slapped me on the face, saying I had become unbearable and demanding that I leave sooner than I planned.

I was so hurt! Was he cheating on me again? With whom? And why? I tried to be the best wife and mother! As usual, I had no answer. Finally, I told him I did not want to leave and that we would leave all together after the baby was born. But Vito did not want to pay the hospital bills and said it would be better for me to be with Mama and deliver the baby at home. At the end I resigned to leaving. Besides, what difference did it make? He had proved over and over that he did not want me. Thinking about the baby in my womb made me cry desperately.

Time was going by fast, and May 15, the day of our

departure was approaching. The night before, Santino had a very high fever, but I was feeling well. Although I was seven-months pregnant, I did not close my eyes the whole night. The few days before had been very stressful as I tried to leave everything in place for my husband. I had also made several new cloth items for me and the boys. That day I was scared out of my wits. Would I be able to do it all by myself?

On the morning of May 15, Santino still had a high fever, and Fabio was sick as well. I pulled myself together and told myself I had to leave. My husband was very happy and did not seem to care about any of my fears. I tried not to think about what I suspected and knew in my heart. He must have cheated on me for some time now, but I was too sick to fight him. Whenever I asked him about it, his answer was the same, "You're crazy!"

The day of my departure, most of my friends came over to say good-bye. Grazia was crying and told me that she would never forget me. I told her that I was thankful for what she had done for me, and I hugged her. Rosa and her mother accompanied me to the airport as well as Giovanna and her husband, Stephen.

When it was time to say the last good-byes, Vito hugged me and told me to stay calm, not to worry about anything, and that he would join me soon. We would then buy a house and stay in Palermo, permanently. Santino and Fabio hugged their papa. Santino cried, but Fabio didn't. I walked to the airplane with Fabio in one arm, a huge bag in the other and Santino holding my skirt. I turned to wave good-bye one more time and then boarded the plane.

The trip was hellish. The kids were both sick with high fevers and crying continuously. They started to throw up, and I didn't know what to do next. I called the flight attendant, but she was not very kind. She refused to give me anything for the kids. I was really worried. Their fevers were high throughout the flight, and I had to change them several times. I will never forget that trip.

When we arrived in Rome, I was exhausted. We had to take a connecting flight to Palermo, and we walked from one terminal to the other. Again I had Fabio in one arm, the huge bag in the other arm, and Santino attached to the bag. I hardly had energy to walk. I almost fell down while boarding the bus that would take us to the other terminal. There were a lot of people at the terminal, but nobody offered to help me. I prayed to God to give me the strength to make it to Palermo. I was feeling as if I had started labor.

With great joy, I found my brother Rino at the airline check-in desk. He was waiting for me, and to my great relief, he took Fabio from one arm and the bag from the other. Oh, what a relief! I thanked him over and over and looked at him as if he were an angel. Rino was happy to see me too. He had just finished his military duty and had gotten engaged to a girl named Dora. He had become a very handsome man with big dark eyes, dark curly hair, and a broad, winning smile. The only thing new on him were glasses, which he had never worn before. Together, we boarded the plane to Palermo, my very dear city.

Chapter 7
Going Back to Italy

After four years away I was back in Italy. How I had dreamed about this moment! I would soon be among people who loved me. Vito was completely out of my mind. All I wanted was to taste the sweetness of those moments.

While the plane was getting ready to land, I took a look at my city, its sea, and its mountains. I was elated. In a few more minutes, my plane would land! Again Rino took Fabio in his arms with my huge bag, while Santino held my hand. While getting off the plane, I saw a large crowd. In the crowd I could easily see Papa. He looked taller than the others. Perhaps he had climbed on something. He was waving his hand, and my heart was filling with love. A knot in my throat almost stopped my breath. I ran toward Papa and hugged him crying. Mama was also crying and gave me the biggest hug. Oh, how good it was to be in her arms again! All my siblings, nieces, and nephews took turns hugging me. Fabio was so scared by all the people that he was clinging to my arms. But Santino was happy to be the center of attention.

I had to live with my in-laws because all my furniture was still at their home. All those years, we had been paying rent for the two rooms. But things would be different this time. I was not going to allow anyone to intimidate me.

I could not believe that I was finally home. It was springtime and Palermo was entirely covered by flowers. Everything seemed to be blooming. There were so many changes, new busy streets, shopping centers, and condominiums. I could hardly believe the changes that has occurred in four short years.

It was so beautiful to be in familiar surroundings again. At Mama's house the jasmine plant had reached the balcony of the third floor and the orange tree had so many blossoms! There were no longer any pumpkin plants, and in their place was a beautiful climbing plant with white and blue flowers. The pomegranate tree had been chopped down, but it was still a nice garden.

I lifted my eyes to the opposite side of the garden, toward Bruno's balcony, and a lump came to my throat. How I had cherished the memories of our innocent love story. I asked Mama if she had any news about Bruno. She said she heard that he had moved to France and married a French woman. I was kind of happy to hear that, and I hoped with all my heart that at least he was happily married.

Vito called me often and sounded very loving. During one conversation, he told me that he had bought a ticket and was arriving on July 28 aboard the *Raffaello* cruise ship. My hopes were rekindled. Perhaps here in Sicily, I could put my family together, as my heart desired. All I had to do until Vito's arrival was concentrate on my pregnancy and the baby's arrival.

Santino easily adjusted to having so many people around him and was happy. On the contrary, Fabio was a shy baby and did not like the crowds. He wanted to constantly be in my arms. During my labor pains, he had to be pulled out of my arms. I could still hear his screams from my delivery room.

It was a home delivery, and I was assisted by Mama, Aurora, my mother-in-law, and the doctor. Rocco was born at 1:30 in the afternoon on July 5. He weighed eleven pounds and looked like a two-month-old baby. He was beautiful with a cute, round face, brown eyes, and dark hair so long that it touched his neckline. Everybody was admiring him, and I was truly happy that God had answered my prayers once again. I wanted another boy, because I feared that a girl would have the same bad luck I had. Looking at the baby, my mother-in-law said, "When your husband finds out you had another boy, he will no longer want to come!" The doctor was still around and said, "Mrs. Avella, what are you talking about? Your son got exactly what he planted!" Embarrassed, she did not open her mouth again.

I called Vito, and he was so happy to have another son. He told me he could not wait to come home. He asked to talk to the kids and told me that he loved me. At last! How I had longed to hear those words! It seemed like going back to the times when Vito had been crazy about me. How was it possible that he didn't love me anymore? Or was it perhaps the hardship of living so far from home. Anyway, I stopped wondering why.

Mama came to visit everyday and spent several hours with me. She always had a smile on her face, which encouraged me. Papa also stopped by everyday after work. I had a good chance to spend time with Aurora and talk about everything that had happened in the States. She was really sorry for me.

During one of his phone calls Vito asked me to come to Naples with his sister Rosetta and her husband, Carlo, to meet him. He did not want me to come alone. I agreed. I left Fabio and Rocco with their grandparents. Santino, Rosetta Carlo, and I left for Naples two days before Vito's ship was scheduled to arrive

Rosetta had friends in Naples. A cheery family hosted us and took us sightseeing around the city. I was happy to revisit the place of my honeymoon, and Santino was elated to play with the family dog. He had made a real friend. It was funny watching Santino chase the poor dog until the poor animal had no energy left. We would all laugh at the games they played. I remember that the host said with a smile: "Next time you come, you may bring one hundred children, but not one Santino." We all laughed.

I was looking forward to seeing my husband. I had chosen to forget all the past events and was looking towards a future with new hopes. I was happy, relaxed, and looking good. I had lost all the weight I gained during my pregnancy. When I looked at myself in the mirror I said, "Not bad!" After three children, I still had the shape of a teenager. My face had regained its natural splendor and my blue eyes shined with joy. I let my curly hair hang loose on my shoulders, like Vito liked it, and wore a red miniskirt with a white blouse. I so wanted my husband to find me sexy.

Santino was wearing blue pants and a lighter tee shirt. He was so impatient to see his papa. We went to the port where we could already see the huge ship coming into the harbor. Right away I saw Vito's little red flag waving through the air. Santino was yelling, "Papa! Papa!" My heart was running madly. Finally, Vito was home. Our host got us a pass to board the ship, so we could meet Vito aboard. We hugged one another with joy, and Vito took us all to see his berthing room. Then, on the way down the stairs, he said, "If we meet anyone I know, please don't say that you are my wife. Just tell that you are my girlfriend." Of course, I thought he was joking and he was just making reference to my youthful appearance. We did meet a woman he knew. When she saw me she said, "What a pretty girl. Is this your wife?" And indeed he answered: "No, she is only my girlfriend!" That really hurt, but I did not want to fight and so I said nothing.

From the *Raffaello* we went to catch a ferry to Palermo. It was late, and we could only find one room. We decided that we would take turns sleeping. Rosetta and Carlo went first, taking Santino with them. Vito and I were finally alone. We had so much to talk about! He told me that he loved me and was happy to be back, but mentioned nothing about the past nor did he apologize. He sounded sincere, and I was happy. We went for a walk on the deck, and he held me in his arms.

The deck was totally deserted, and he kissed me passionately. I remembered the exact same moments on the same ship, during our honeymoon. The moon was splendid just like that night, and I could see the stars in the clear, dark waters. Everything was perfect, and I thanked God for having given me my husband back.

Our moment of romance was broken when Vito realized that he had left his suit bag in the lounge. We rushed there and found it still on the couch. Thank God! In the pocket of one suit was our entire life savings. It was a miracle that we found it still there and intact.

We decided to stay in the lounge when suddenly a lady, who seemed to know Vito, came to sit with us. She started chatting with him in a friendly way and after a few minutes, Vito introduced me. "Oh, this is my girlfriend!" I quickly replied, "You know he is joking, we are married and have three kids!" The lady looked at me with a sad expression and said, "I am sorry for you, Miss. But I must tell you, that during the trip from America, your husband spent his days with a woman called Rosina." I was dumbfounded.

Looking toward my husband, the woman exclaimed, "Aren't you ashamed, Vito? With such a pretty wife, how could you do that?" Vito, took a deep breath and said, "It was nothing more than friendship." Shaking her head, the lady said good-bye and left. Back in the room, I asked him more questions. He swore that he had told the truth, and I desperately wanted to believe him.

The following day when we arrived in Palermo, the port was filled with all kinds of relatives and friends. Rosa and her mother, who had arrived the day before by plane, where there. Fabio was very happy to see me, and Rocco, who was now a month old, was sleeping quietly. Vito saw his third son for the first time and said, "I thought you were exaggerating, but you are right, he really is huge and beautiful!" Vito was beaming with joy and Rocco had an expression on his face that looked like he was smiling back at him.

The days that followed were full of planning. Vito wanted to buy a tobacco shop and started looking for one. We also decided to have Rocco baptized, which required a lot of planning. After the baptism ceremony Vito wanted to have a big party with lots of music and dancing.

We chose a restaurant in Montelepre, which was owned by Rosa's future in-laws. Despite all of our efforts to have a joyful celebration, the evening was a flop. For some reason everyone looked sad and bored. Curious, I asked, "Mama why do look so sad?" Her reply was that she was tired.

After the party Rosa asked us to come visit her the next day in Montelepre. Paolo, her fiancee, was still in the military and would return a week before the wedding. In the meantime, she did not feel too comfortable with his parents and wanted company. Vito and I were happy to help out and visited her everyday for nearly six weeks. One day Rosa confided to me that she really did not love Paolo but felt she could not back out of the marriage. "Everything is ready," she said, as if trying to convince herself, rather than me. "But it is not right!," I said. Rosa's only response was tears of sorrow. I felt sorry for her. It was hard to see her so sad. Everyday she rehashed the same story. Finally I talked to Vito about it, and he agreed with me.

Paolo was a very nice young man, tall and skinny with dark straight hair and big dark eyes. He looked very intelligent. He met Rosa during a trip to New York, and they became engaged. He had returned to Italy to fulfill his military duties, and they would not see each other again until their wedding day.

On the morning of the wedding, I left little Rocco with Aurora. Vito, Santino and I were all in the wedding party. Vito was the best man, Santino was the ring bearer, and I was the matron of honor. Santino looked so handsome with his black pants and white shirt. Vito, who was wearing a black tuxedo, looked very sharp. Fabio, who wore a white suit with gold trim, looked like a little angel. I wore a green chiffon dress with a matching hat.

As matron of honor, I had to help the bride get ready. Rosa was staying at the home of Paolo's uncle, so I went there, while my husband went to Paolo's house. I helped her get dressed and fix her veil. She looked really sad, and again I reminded her that she still had time to back out. But again, she said no, that it was too late.

Vito was outside, waiting with a car. He looked at her with very sad eyes. At that very moment, my eyes opened. "My husband was in love with Rosa!," I thought. I felt a sharp pain, that felt like a knife going through my heart. Could my husband be having an affair with my best friend? Was I so blind all this time? I would ask him after the wedding, but I already knew his answer, "You're a crazy woman." Was I really crazy to suspect his infidelity all the time?

Rosa was married at a small church in the mountains of Montelepre. Rosa sadly uttered, "I do," and the ceremony was finally over. From appearances it was a nice wedding ceremony, but in my heart I knew the ugly truth. Rosa did not love her husband; she loved my husband.

At the reception, Vito sat right next to Rosa and behaved like he was the bridegroom. Paolo and I sat next to Vito and Rosa in utter amazement. Vito danced only with Rosa, while I sat alone. Rosa ignored me and took a lot of pictures with Vito. Paolo looked very nervous, but like me, he said nothing. Even the guests seemed to notice that something was wrong. The groom and I must have looked like two idiots standing next to Vito and Rosa as they posed for picture after picture.

After the awkward reception, we accompanied the bride and groom to Palermo's Grand Hotel, a seaside hotel next to the seaport, and returned home. I did not have any time to speak to Vito alone. When we arrived home I was so sick that

I fell on the bed. I have no idea why or what happened next.

The following day I got up and felt quite rested. I did not remember a thing about the wedding. I felt happy and so in love with my husband. Together we took the newlyweds to the port. At the seaport we all hugged and said good-bye, promising that when Rosa and Paolo returned we would all take a trip together. During our drive home, Vito seemed quiet, but I did not pay much attention.

The week following Rosa's wedding was calm. The children were happy in Palermo, and even Fabio had gotten used to having so many people around. He was still pretty much attached to me, especially when I held Rocco in my arms. But I did my best to spend as much time as possible with him. Santino was so busy with all his cousins, that he was not at all jealous of the attention I gave Fabio or Rocco. Rocco always seemed to be hungry. Vito was happy too, but he was growing tired of looking for a tobacco shop to buy. "You will come across something," I said trying to assure him.

When the newlyweds returned from their honeymoon, they looked cheerful. Rosa gave Vito a big hug, and also hugged me and the children. The next day we were all ready for our trip together. Rosa's mother joined us, and we also took Santino. My sister Aurora kept Fabio and Rocco.

I was so excited, thinking that the trip would be a second honeymoon for Vito and me. However, it was a total disaster. Throughout the trip, I could not spend one night alone with Vito because Rosa kept insisting that she was sick and needed my attention. Strangely, I always agreed to help her. It was all so strange. Whenever it dawned on me that something was wrong and I wanted to talk it over with Vito, I always felt sick and forgot what I was about to say. Everyday I acted like a little puppy following Vito around. What made things even stranger was that the same thing was happening to Rosa's husband. Paolo was always feeling sick, yet affectionate toward his wife.

When we returned to Palermo, Paolo's parents were very upset, claiming they had found white powder and other strange things under the mattress of the beds where Rosa and her mother had slept. To my surprise, they accused Rosa and her mother of practicing witchcraft. Then Rosa and her mother began to accuse them of the same things.

There was a big fight. The in-laws claimed they noticed something strange on the wedding day. Rosa and her mother denied everything. Then Paolo started screaming at Rosa, accusing her of having an affair with Vito. Silently, I witnessed his accusations toward my husband who, like Rosa, denied everything. Paolo kept screaming until he passed out.

Vito and I got in the car to leave. As we drove away, I started accusing Vito of having an affair. Again he said I was crazy. I too passed out, but Vito did not even stop the car. When I regained consciousness, I felt so rested and happy. I hugged Vito, not remembering ever arguing.

A week after the fiasco at Paolo's parents house everyone was scattered. Paolo had to go back to finish his military duties. Rosa and her mother returned to New York to begin the paperwork for Paolo's visa. Vito and I stayed in Palermo. Despite the accusations, I went to the airport to see Rosa off. Before she boarded the plane, I hugged her very warmly and told her that I still loved her.

After Rosa's departure, Vito seemed annoyed, as if he had no peace. He kept saying he did not want to stay in Palermo because he had not found the right business to invest in. He insisted we return to the United States, but I refused to leave.

Arguing with Vito proved to be useless, like talking to the wind. To my surprise, my father-in-law started arguing with Vito too. He tried to convince him to stay in Palermo, claiming to know "the true reason" Vito wanted to go back to the States. "Its not for any business, but to follow Rosa," he said. Vito denied the accusations, sticking to his story about not finding a business to invest in. Finally his father looked at me and said, "You are stupid! This story has been going on for years. How can you be so blind?" I was speechless, as if I had heard it for the first time. Vito continued to deny his father's accusations, saying they were all envious of his friendship with Rosa and her mother.

When we were alone, I asked Vito again about his relationship with Rosa. He claimed rumors of an affair with Rosa were all lies. Looking at me, he said he was leaving for the States and it was up to me whether of not I wanted to join him. He did not seem care about my decision.

The days that followed were hellish. What could I to do? I wanted to keep my family together. But if Vito started treating me badly, as he had before, what would I do? Mama tried to comfort me and encouraged me to leave with my husband.

Amidst accusations, arguments, and confusion, I started preparing for yet another departure. I had longed so much to return to Palermo. I had thought here I could have had the family I always dreamed of. However, fate had been against me, and my return to Palermo was turning into a total fiasco. Heartbroken, I decided to pick up the pieces of my shattered dreams and to return to the States with Vito.

How would I survive solitude again? My heart was bleeding. I decided to visit Sister Maria again. I wanted to take refuge in the chapel and find a little peace. But a big surprise was in store. Sister Francesca came to meet me and said, "I am so sorry, Anna, Sister Maria has left us to be with Jesus." I was stunned. My dear Sister Maria was no longer. Her beautiful smile, her melodious voice, her wonderful words, all were gone! I went to the chapel and cried my heart out. That place had always been medicine for my spirit. I looked around and tried to memorize everything, to be able to take that peace with myself and my decision. I said good-bye to all the nuns and returned home. I felt at peace with myself, although I saddened by the news of Sister Maria's death.

We started planning our departure for November 1, 1973. Again, our entry into the States would be through Canada, because we still did not have proper visas. But this time there was another problem. Fabio, who had been born in the States, had an American passport which would create a problem. We decided to leave him in Palermo. A cousin, who would be traveling to New York, would bring him to us.

I was sad. Of all people how could I leave Fabio? He was literally attached to me. Would he get sick? How long would it be before I would be with my whole family again. My family had grown so big! There were so many kids. Papa looked at me with tears in his eyes. My children were very attached to grandpa Aldo. He played with them, the same way that he had played with me. Always holding them in his arms, teasing, and asking over and over, "Do you love me?"

When the dreaded day I arrived, I really cried. Fabio was peacefully sleeping in his bed as I gently kissed him. I felt a sharp pain in my heart and I tried to cry softly, so I would not to wake him up. If he were awake, I would not have the strength to leave him. I slowly left his room to join Vito, Santino, and Rocco.

As we arrived at the airport Santino was feeling excited about going for a ride on the airplane, and Rocco was sleeping quietly in my arms. My whole family went with us to the airport. Still crying, I hugged everyone, especially Papa, and Mama. Vito was holding Santino's hand, and I had Rocco in my arms. We boarded the plane, and as we were going up the steps, I turned around. Once again I saw Papa waving his hand and once again I said good-bye to my beloved Palermo. During our flight to Canada, I thought about my dreams and hopes. They had all been broken.

Chapter 8
Looking Toward The Future

We were finally on the plane for Canada. The children slept quietly, and even Vito was napping. But I could not rest. Too many thoughts crowded my mind. I was not happy. I hoped with all my heart that my husband would love and respect me. I tried to focus only on good things. I just wanted a happy family, that was the only thing I wanted. Was it possible that my husband did not have the same wishes?

When we arrived in Canada, everything was pretty much the same. Lots of phone calls, meeting people we did not know, sleeping in motels, long bus rides, traveling at night on back roads, smuggling ourselves back into New York.

This time we went to Queens to live with my sister-in-law, Giovanna. Weeks later, Vito found an apartment in Brooklyn, right around the corner from Rosa's. The apartment was on the third floor of a very old building. There were two bedrooms, a living room, dining room, small kitchen, and bathroom. Again Vito brought basic furnishings and started working again.

Fabio, who was now three-years-old, joined us a month after we arrived. I was so happy to have my baby back in my arms! As soon as he saw me, he attached himself to me and would not let go. He kept telling me he loved me. Santino, who had missed him a lot, was happy to have his little brother back.

Rosa and her mother came to visit us every day. I tried to pay close attention to her behavior, watching how she would interact with Vito. "My God those two look in love!," I thought. I tried to talk to Vito about Rosa, but his answer was that I was crazy and should have stayed in Palermo.

Vito worked at night and slept during the day. In the afternoons he would go out, unless, of course, Rosa came to visit. Then, he would stay at home. I was feeling physically sick. Sometimes I did not even have the strength to take care of the kids. One day, in a moment of rage, I threw Rosa out of the apartment, telling her exactly what I suspected. She said there was nothing going on and it was just my imagination. I insisted that I did not want to see her again, because she had broken our friendship.

A couple of hours later, Vito came home. He knew everything about my argument with Rosa. We argued for a while and then he hit me right in front of the kids. Frightened the kids started screaming. Vito told me that if I wanted to live in America, I had to be quiet, otherwise I'd better begin packing my suitcases. Then, he picked me up and carried me outside, leaving me by the front door. He then locked me out.

The kids continued to scream, as I banged on the door begging Vito to let me in. But he refused to open it. I stopped banging when I heard Santino yelling, "Papa, open the door, or I will call the police!" Vito opened the door. When I walked in Santino was still holding the telephone in his hand. Santino and Fabio ran toward me and hugged me, while little Rocco lay crying in his crib. Vito left the house and did not come back home that night.

After three days, I called my mother-in-law, who had come to America the week before, because Giovanna was having a baby. I explained that Vito had not come home for three days. She and Stephen, Giovanna's husband, found out where Vito was staying, and came to see me. She wanted to bring Vito with her, but I told her that if he was going to continue his ways, he'd better stay where he was. "So it is you who wants to leave my son," she replied. I couldn't believe her words.

Stephen convinced me to take Vito back. Vito came home, but for almost a month we did not speak to each other. When we finally started talking again, it seemed our marriage was really over. Vito did not come home except to sleep. It was as if I did not exist. There was no conversation, no love, only putting up with each other. He seldom wanted to have sex, and when he did, I felt as was as if he used me and threw me away. I had no contact with anyone. The only person who came to visit was my friend, Grazia. I did not tell Mama because she would have been angry. Writing Aurora was my only way of venting my frustrations during those terrible months.

Rosa never came back to my house, but I sensed that she was still seeing my husband. When Paolo finished his stint in the military, he came to America.

When he arrived in New York, Rosa admitted that she did not love him and told him she wanted a divorce. Paolo was devastated. Unmoved, Rosa called the police and had him thrown out.

Vito and I continued to fight. I knew in my heart he was still seeing Rosa. He would leave in the afternoon and come back at four in the morning. I was so depressed! I often thought about leaving him, but then I would change my mind. Where would I go with three kids? I had nowhere to turn.

One night Vito did not come back home, and I, like an idiot, was worried about him. The next day he walked in the apartment happy and cheerful. But I blew up, and we had a big fight. He told me that the door was open and that I could leave whenever I wanted to. He told me to leave him alone. I called Stephen and asked him to talk to Vito. I needed to know if Vito wanted to stay married or not.

After his talk with Vito, things seemed to improve a little.

He went out less, and when he had a free day, he spent it with me and the kids. Then he started inviting his friends to the house. They would stay up drinking and playing cards until the early hours of the morning. I was not happy, but put up with it, just to have Vito at home.

After eight months in that apartment, I convinced Vito to move. The apartment building had become a mess. Kids who looked like they were strung out on drugs were hanging all over the staircase. They would often sleep right behind our door. I was alone with the boys at night, and often scared. So we found a new apartment, with four rooms and a large basement. It was on the same street where we had lived four years earlier. In that house the kids would have a bit more space to play.

When we moved Rocco already walked by himself and was beginning to learn his first words. He was so lovely to look at; tall and big, he always looked older than he was. Santino had started school, and Fabio, always attached to my apron, would never let me out of his sight. Life was quite monotonous. Vito continued with his old ways, and again I was alone with the kids.

Grazia had moved out of the neighborhood and had found a job so she rarely came over to visit. An old Italian couple lived next door. The wife, Mrs. Marta, was very nice and we became friends. She was like a mother to me and I began to feel comfortable confiding in her and telling her about my problems. I thanked God that I had found another mother.

When Rocco was two years old, we finally got a chance to make our residency papers official, so that we could apply for green cards. Vito had a regular job contract. There was only one problem. In order to get a regular visa, we had to go to an American consulate in Italy. All paperwork had to be processed in Palermo.

I was very happy. I would have a chance to see my beloved

family again. We started preparing for the trip home, which would take place on January 11, 1975. We arrived in Palermo on the twelfth, our eighth wedding anniversary. It was not long since I had been in Palermo, but all the same, I was very emotional. When the plane was getting ready to land, my heart began to pound, as I my beloved city came into view. As usual, Papa was the first one to spot me and hug me. Mama and I began to weep for joy. My whole family and Vito's family were there. It was so nice to see them all.

Mama noticed right away that there was something wrong. She began questioning me. Finally, in a fit of tears, I told her everything I had gone through, except the beatings. Mama was astonished. She could not believe what Vito had put me through. Where had all his love gone? She said that she would tell Papa, and together, they would talk to Vito. I begged her not to do it, fearing it would make things worse for me. But Mama did not want to hear it, and together with Papa, she spoke to Vito.

As usual, Vito said that I was crazy. He denied doing anything wrong, and accused me of being too jealous, claiming it was the reason we were constantly fighting. He told them he loved me and promised that he would try to do his best to treat me better. During our forty-five day stay in Palermo, he was very affectionate, and again a little hope was rekindled in my heart. But I began to notice that although Vito did his best to show my parents that he loved me, when we were at his parents' house he treated me badly.

Time went by very fast and thank God we got all the necessary paperwork done. We were now legal residents of the United States. Vito was very happy, but I did not want to return to my new country. I tried to find excuses to spend as much time as possible with my family. When our departure date arrived, I was smiling, but within me I was crying. I would continue again that lonely and unhappy life, far away from my family. I kept telling myself that this was my fate.

Again, the last person I saw before boarding the plane was Papa. His beloved figure always remained impressed in my memory and reminded me of all the people I loved. This time the trip was easy, straight to New York. The kids would not go to sleep during the eight-hour flight. They kept me so busy, I did not have time to think.

A few weeks after we got back, I received a phone call that surprised me. It was Rosa's mother, who was calling to tell me that Rosa was very sick. She asked me if Vito was at home and could bring her to the doctor. I said no, but she kept pressing me. Vito was listening to the conversation and before I finished talking, he was ready to go pick up Rosa. I tried to stop him, but he was very worried. I told him that if he was going, I was going too. So we left the boys with Mrs. Marta and rushed to Rosa's apartment.

When we arrived Rosa was in bed complaining of she had stomach cramps. Vito and her mother raised her out of the bed and helped her outside. Then they put her in the passenger's seat of the car, naturally, next to my husband. Then we drove to the emergency room of Brooklyn General Hospital. I told Vito to go home; I would stay with Rosa. But he was very concerned and said he wanted to know what the doctor had to say.

While I was talking to Vito, Rosa's mother came over and said the doctor needed to speak with Vito, because Rosa was too sick to talk, and she did not speak English. They left me in the waiting room and went into the emergency room with Rosa.

After four hours, Rosa was released from the emergency room, and we drove her home. She insisted that she still had pain, but she looked good and was even in a good mood. Her mother also was in a good mood and was chatting with Vito. She told Vito to go get the boys and she would cook for everybody. We would have supper together. Vito went to Mrs. Marta's to pick up the children, while I said absolutely nothing. I felt as if I were tied up, especially after drinking the coffee. It had a really bitter taste, unlike the expresso that I was accustomed to drinking. When I asked about the taste, Rosa's mother said that she had switched brands. Suddenly, I felt like my head was spinning. Then I began to feel very fond of Rosa. I hugged her with the promise that I would visit her again and often.

From that day a new routine began. I went to visit Rosa every day, and every Sunday we all went out together. My husband and I never left the house alone. We were inseparable, and strangely enough I did not even mind or remember any of the past events. The kids grew very fond of Rosa. She was very kind to them and me. I loved her with all my heart. She had moved and now lived right across the street from us. Every Sunday, when Vito came back from work, we were all ready to go to the beach. It was summer, and the heat and humidity in New York were unbearable. But the kids were so very happy. For the first time, since we had come to the States, we went out almost every Sunday.

It was as if my life changed. I used to always stay home with the boys. But now, we were going out every Sunday. In a few months I saw more than I had seen in all my life in America. Vito took us to see the Statue of Liberty. Naturally Rosa and her mother always went with us. We were just one big family.

Mama would write to me to ask if everything was fine. I always answered yes. Papa was ill, with diabetes, and I was worried about him. Whenever Vito allowed me, I called him just to hear his voice and reassure myself that he was okay.

One day Vito bought tickets for all of us to go on a cruise ship. The ship would sail all around New York and stop at an amusement park at Rye Beach. The trip was organized by an Italian club and featured lots of Italian music and games. Vito tried to convince me to stay at home, claiming it would not be suitable for the children, but I insisted on going.

When the day of our cruise arrived, it was raining. But since he had already bought the tickets, we decided to go. I prepared a lot of different foods to take with us for a picnic. Once aboard the ship, I was really happy although I had three kids to keep an eye on, while Vito was running all around the ship. Then Rosa left me with the kids with the excuse that she had to look for a friend. Hours went by, and it was still raining. Finally, I asked Rosa's mother to watch the kids, and I decided to go look for Vito. The crowd was big, and it was not easy to find anyone. I stopped on the deck where there was a band playing, and spotted Vito and Rosa dancing cheek to cheek. I stood watching them, motionless. For a moment I thought they saw me, but perhaps they did not because they continued their romantic dance. Frustrated and crying, I went back to where I had left the kids. I said nothing to Rosa's mother. After a short while, Vito and Rosa came back, calm and cool, as if nothing had happened. I was completely silent, not a word came out of my mouth.

The ship finally stopped. But due to the rain, no one was allowed to get off. Rosa complained that she had to go to the bathroom and that she did not feel well. The bathrooms on the ship were already closed, but she argued so much that they let her off. Five minutes later Vito did the same thing. One hour went by and there was no sign of either of them. When it stopped raining, everyone else got off the ship. Rosa's mother had met some friends, and the kids and I began looking for Vito. I walked throughout the whole park, but did not see him anywhere.

I was really upset. I began crying, confused about where to go or what to do. I was disgusted! The kids were getting hungry, so I stopped to get something for them to eat. I met some people I knew, and I sat close to them, as if looking for support. We spent many hours in the park; there were carrousels, and many games for the children. Everybody was having fun, except me. I was full of worries and fears. I kept glancing toward the ship longing to leave.

Right before our scheduled departure, Rosa and Vito walked up to me. They yelled at me saying they had been looking for me all day. My husband demanded to know where I had been. "I have been sitting here at this stupid table all day long!," I said. In front of everyone, he called me an idiot and a good-for-nothing, and said I should have stayed at home. Confused, angry, and tired, I wished I had stayed home.

Life went on as usual. Rosa was always at my house, and every night, as soon as she walked in, Vito would send me to put the kids to bed. I listened to him like a puppy. Coming back to the kitchen, I would see them engaged in very personal conversations, but did not think much of it. I would have moments of awareness, and moments of total obscurity. Whenever my wits were with me, I would tell my husband that I did not want Rosa in the house, but after a while I would call her and invite her over. Mrs. Marta, who was not as blind as I was, would often say, "Open your eyes, my dear!" But I would tell her that everything was fine and I felt rather happy.

Vito was very detached from the kids and they suffered, especially Santino who was very attached to Vito. Santino's heart was filled with sadness, as a result he was not doing well in school. I tried by best to help him, but was unsuccessful. He was in second grade and not very happy about going to school. One morning while I was preparing to walk him to school, he decided to run away from me. I was very scared. I called Vito and left Rocco and Fabio with Mrs. Marta.

I went to the school thinking, "Who knows, perhaps he wanted to go alone." But he was not there. My fears increased, and while walking back home, I prayed with all my heart. When I opened the door I found him at home, crying and yelling that he did not like going to school. "You have no choice. All kids must go to school," I explained.

When Vito came home, he was out of his mind with rage. He did not say a word nor did he allow me to say a word. He grabbed Santino, lifted him up and pushed him down the basement stairs. I screamed with all my strength, as I pushed Vito out of the way. Rushing into the basement, I feared I would find Santino dead. When Santino began to cry I thanked God that he was still alive. He did not have one single scratch, but was crying his heart out in shock. Watching from the basement door, Vito rushed down into the basement and, in a fury, pulled Santino out of my arms. He tied him to a pole with a rope, turned the light off, and pulled me upstairs by the hair. Santino was screaming, "Mama, Mama, I am scared!" I tried to free myself from Vito's grasp and run downstairs, but he was holding me tightly. I punched and kicked him, but he did the same to me.

I swore to Vito that if anything happened to that child, I would kill him. Then he let me go, but did not allow me to go to Santino. Finally he went to bed. I rushed down the basement immediately and untied my child. I held him to my heart, and we both cried. Santino was shaking like a leaf. I carried him upstairs and washed his face with cold water. Then I tried to calm him down and feed him something. He laid in bed for the rest of the day, with a sad expression on his face.

From that day on I blamed Rosa for Vito's neglect of the boys and me. I promised myself that I would no longer allow that woman in my house. But the promise did not last. That same night, I felt this incredible love towards her which even today, after twenty-two years, I cannot explain it. So I cooked supper, and I invited her to come over, as if nothing had happened. Many days went on like this. I would argue with Vito blaming Rosa for his attitude toward the kids; but unable to stand up to Rosa, I still asked her to come over.

Then one day I was so sick that I did not have the energy to get out of bed. I could not even open my eyes or feel my body. It was as if I were almost paralyzed. I was as if in coma, a really strange feeling. I could hear the kids screaming in the kitchen and my husband yelling at them. Then I heard him call Rosa and ask her to come and take care of his children. She came over immediately and cooked breakfast for everybody. I was dozing, but I overheard my husband say, "Santino, if Mama dies, whom do you want for a Mama?" He answered, "ROSA." He asked Fabio and Rocco the same question. And both their answers were the same, "ROSA."

I felt something rebelling inside of me, and I began to cry. I tried to open my eyes, I had to. What would have happened to my children? I prayed and prayed, "My God, help me, please. I don't want to die. My children need me. I don't want to leave them in their hands!" I felt stronger, and I asked Vito to take me to the hospital. Santino cried, "NO, Mama, no!" So I asked him to drive me to a church instead. I could speak! My voice was back! Vito and Rosa looked at me surprised. So I said I wanted to go to a church in the Bronx, where there was holy water and the Blessed Sacrament.

They seemed annoyed, but helped me into the car since I could not walk. We drove to a church, and they walked me over to where the holy water was. My legs were shaking, and I fell on my knees. I cried and began to pray. Tears were running down my face. I don't even know how long I spent there. Vito, Rosa and the kids went for a walk in the park near the church. When they came back, I was still on my knees. I felt better, though. I got up and started laughing for joy. I was feeling better. I looked toward heaven and thanked God. The kids were very happy, but Vito and Rosa looked astonished and seemed upset.

Vito did not ask a question or utter a word. We went back home, and life continued as usual. I despised Rosa, but

I also invited her to the house. I would cook for her and, like a marionette, every night I would leave her alone with Vito while I put the boys to bed. I often had excruciating headaches, as if someone were putting pins in my head. Although I was taking aspirins, they did not help.

One day Rosa said, "Why don't we get our hair cut short?" We both had long hair. Her hair was long and straight, and mine long and curly. I told her that I did not want to cut my hair because Vito liked me with long hair. But the next day, I called her and invited her to go with me to the hairdresser. At the beauty shop, Rosa said, "Okay, best if you go first, because Mama can't watch your kids for long." I agreed, and while the hair stylist was chopping my hair off, she said she had to run and get a soda. But she did not come back. Afterwards she said that she had to run some errands and had forgotten to come back. So I went home with a crew-cut, while she still had her shining, long hair.

Vito did not even notice that my pretty hair was gone! In fact, he never seemed to notice anything about me. We slept in the same bed, but did not have sex for months. I did not care. I had so much washing, ironing, and cooking to do. I took care of a house for three kids, my husband, Rosa, and her mother. I had no time to care about anything. I thought that things were going well, but since my return to New York, I had lost a lot of weight, and had no appetite at all.

On Christmas 1975, Vito's brother, Sarino, came from Italy. With him were his wife and a set of two-year-old twins, Marzia and Lucia. They were staying with us until Sarino found a job, and they could get a place of their own.

While they lived at our apartment, Rosa came over regularly, but not everyday. One day Sarino approached me and said, "Anna, what's going on? I see some strange things happening. Is it possible that you are not aware of anything?" I told him how strange I felt. Some days I would hate Rosa and some days I would love her. And then I told him the whole story of what had happened, and how his brother was behaving toward me and the kids. My brother-in-law spoke to Vito, but the results were disastrous. They argued for hours.

Encouraged by Sarino, I did not let Rosa come into my house any longer, and I called my sister Aurora. I told Aurora that I suspected Rosa and her mother had some strange powers over me. Aurora was horrified and wanted to know why I had not called sooner. "I don't know. All I know is that woman has power over me. One day I hate her guts, and the next day, I love her to death." I explained.

Chapter 9
Encounter with a Sorceress

I told Rosa that I did not want to see her any longer, but she continued to see Vito anyway. She also kept on calling me and even knocked at the door. She refused to give up, but I was in a lucid state of mind and prepared to fight back. I had headaches and felt sick, but I was firm in rejecting her.

One morning my sister Aurora called me and told me that I had to go back to Sicily. She said that my life was in danger, and I did not have long to live. She had consulted a sorceress who recommended that I come back to Palermo immediately.

I was in a great state of confusion. How could I leave so soon? And how would I explain things to Vito? Together with my brother-in-law, I found the perfect excuse. I would tell Vito that my father was really sick, and that I had to leave immediately. When I told Vito he did not say a word, but looked sad. He had not spoken to me in weeks.

I called a travel agency and booked two tickets, one for me and one for Rocco. My sister-in-law offered to watch Santino and Fabio. I planned to leave the following day. With great confusion in my mind, I started packing. I was sad because I did not want to leave my boys, but I had to do it. The next morning when Vito came home from work, he was upset. "Liar! I called your Mama and found out that Papa is doing just fine!," he announced. Mama was of course unaware of my plan, and had told him the truth. Desperate, I told him the real reason why I was going.

"You are crazy!," he yelled, as he grabbed me by the hair pulling me towards him. He raised his hand to hit me, but Sarino stopped him. His brother's intervention made him even more upset, and he became so infuriated that he started punching Sarino who was desperately trying to hold him. When he got free from his brother's hold, he tried to grab me again. The two brothers punched each other a couple of times, and then Sarino pulled Vito into the other room, to get him away from me. My boys were screaming and huddling around me. It felt as if an earthquake had hit the house.

From the other room Vito kept yelling that I was crazy and that I was ruining the reputation of Rosa, claiming she was more honest that I had ever been. When he finally calmed down, he started crying like a baby. Feeling sorry for him, I walked over to him and gave him a hug. "I am sorry for everything," he said.

That afternoon Rocco and I left for Sicily. Santino and Fabio were crying, because they were really scared. I tried to comfort them and told them that grandpa Aldo was sick, and I would be gone for only three weeks. They seemed to calm down a bit, so I left.

The arrival in Palermo was sadder that usual. As always Papa was the first one to greet me. All my family was at the airport with him. Papa looked very sad. In fact, my whole family was sad, and they all tried to comfort me. Even my-in-laws felt the misery that I was going through. Especially sad was my father-in-law, who immediately bought a ticket and left for New York the following day.

That same day Aurora and my brother Angelo took me to see a woman named Mrs. Rosalia, who was going to undo the spell that Rosa and her mother had put on me. According to this woman, Rosa wanted me to die so she could marry Vito.

Mrs. Rosalia was a very beautiful woman, who appeared to be about fifty-five. She was very tall, with big blue eyes, a very rosy complexion, and wore her light brown hair tied up, on the back of her head. I went to see her every day, and my mother-in-law went with me, although her presence made me feel uncomfortable. Mrs. Rosalia and I both believed that she came with me for fear that the sorceress would put a spell on Vito.

One day Mrs. Rosalia told her, "My dear lady, your son is a cruel man. He deserves to die for all the pain he has put this girl through. You must thank God that Anna loves him and wants to forgive him." "You need not come!," she added. From that day on, Vito's mother let me meet with Mrs. Rosalia alone.

Mrs. Rosalia started a therapy for me. She would burn herbs in my presence, making all kinds of signs with her hands all over my body. She would say some strange words and made me repeat them too. She liked me a lot, and every time I went, she would hug me and reassure me that all would be well and my husband would come back to me. She kept saying that my husband would leave the other woman in the near future and come back to me. I felt more relaxed.

After two weeks of this therapy, one night Mrs. Rosalia told me that Rosa's mother had realized why I had gone to Italy. She was trying to work hard on the spell she had on Vito by feeding him all kinds of special foods. Therefore, I needed a stronger dose of medicines to counteract his effects. She asked me to bring to her some gold objects. That same night I called New York and found out that Rosa's mother had invited Vito to dinner twice, and that he had accepted the invitations.

The following day, my whole family, including my grandma, collected some gold objects for me to take to Mrs. Rosalia. The sorceress melted the gold objects and put the liquid in a little bottle. Then she instructed me to break the bottle at midnight, in a crossroads, and to say some lines which I had to memorize.

Anxiously waiting for the time, I followed her instructions and waited to see what would happen. In the morning, a smiling Mrs. Rosalia told me that the experiment had been successful, and that I could go back to New York with nothing to worry about. I sighed a breath of relief, and I thanked and hugged Mrs. Rosalia. I promised her that I would write to announce the results. To show me how much she cared for me, she gave me a password to her. If ever I needed her, all I had to do was repeat the password and she would be right there next to me.

A couple of days later I went back to New York full of hopes and anxieties. I kept telling myself that I had to forget the past and start anew. I had to fall in love with my husband. I had to be able to somehow get my family back together.

Through all those years of unhappiness and solitude, I sometimes thought about Bruno. I wondered whether he was happy. I dreamed about him quite frequently, and in my dreams he was always sick and calling my name. That dream made me sad, so I prayed for him, hoping it was only my bad dream. I wished him happiness. When I was in Sicily, I had asked Mama again about him, and she had said that she knew nothing more than what I knew. His whole family now lived in France.

My return home was a big celebration for my children. They kept hugging me and telling me how much they loved me. Vito came to the airport to pick me up, and he looked more relaxed and even anxious to be alone with me. He did not ask me anything about my trip, and I did not say anything to him.

Life at home started calmly; Vito was going out less and spent more time with the kids. My father-in-law went back to Sicily for a few months, but came back with his wife. They came to live with us. I was not too thrilled about it, but to keep the peace I did not say anything.

I was sewing clothes at home, but after my in-laws arrived I decided to find a job again. Santino and Fabio were in school all day, and Rocco would not be a big problem for his grandma.

I found a job at a factory and was working really hard. I got up at five in the morning, worked in the basement until seven, then I got the children ready for school, walked them to school, and took a bus or train to the factory. I came back home at 5:00 p.m., cooked, cleaned, put the kids to bed, and went to the basement to sew.

As in nature, the calm preceded the storm. Vito converted back to his old ways, going out at night and coming home the next morning. Again my hopes collapsed. Rosa did not live across the street any longer, but nevertheless, she would drive in front of our house every day. One day I noticed that she signaled something to Vito who was sitting outside. I realized that they had never stopped seeing each other. Once I asked Vito about her, and he yelled, "Are you starting again with your crazy thoughts?" As usual my mother-in-law sided with Vito, suggesting that it would be better for all of us, if I calmed down.

One morning while Vito was sleeping and the kids were with their grandparents, I went outside to pick up the mail. I saw Rosa anxiously walking back and forth in front of my door, like a desperate woman. I got upset and yelled out, "If you are waiting for my husband, you'd better be going. He is not home." Rosa became furious. She started insulting me, so I closed the door in her face. As the door was shutting, she yelled that she would call the police.

My in-laws heard the commotion and were upset with me. They left my house for fear that the police would really come. Thank goodness Rosa's outburst did not awaken Vito. He was still sleeping.

After a short while I heard a knock at the door, and it was indeed the police. They said that they had been called by a Mrs. Rosa Bianco who claimed that I had insulted her and damaged her reputation. I was stunned. That hideous woman had turned things completely around. With my broken English, I tried to explain what happened. When the two policemen left, I felt so agitated. The whole day I pondered what to do about Rosa. My in-laws came back that night and did not say a word.

The following morning when Vito came back from work he beat the hell out of me! He said I was ruining his life. I tried to explain what had happened, but he had already heard Rosa's version and he believed her. My in-laws were there, but they did nothing to stop their son from hitting me. Thank God Santino and Fabio, who were at school, were spared from watching my beating. Rocco, however, was at home and cried hysterically.

Emotionally and physically bruised, I decided that I was tired of it all. I told Vito he could do whatever he pleased. I was really tired of him and his parents. I could not bear the burden any longer. From then on, I dedicated my life only to my children. My husband came and left as he pleased. When he had a day off, he usually spent it away from home.

My mother-in-law had also become totally unbearable. She would look at Santino, who was very vivacious, and say, "Your son will end up just like your brother: in jail!" That broke my heart, and I would pray to God, "Lord, I will take anything you send my way. I will take any physical abuse from Vito, but please spare my kids and protect them. Make them grow up to be good and honest men." That was my daily prayer.

Whenever I had a free moment I would go visit Mrs. Marta, just to vent a little. I was very unhappy and lonely. I kept wondering what was wrong with me. Why didn't my husband love me? I was a pretty woman, a good mother, a good cook, why could he not appreciate me? Why did he still love Rosa, who was so fat and ugly and could not do a thing? Those questions always kept running through my mind and I often shared them with Mrs. Marta, who would say, "Honey, stop thinking all those things. It is not your fault. It is he who cannot appreciate what he has!" When I calmed down, I could easily see that my marriage had lasted exactly nineteen months, after that it was one disaster after the other.

Then I would start wondering, "Why did Vito marry me? Had he ever loved me?" My answers were honest. He had married me only because I had rejected him for so long. He knew I loved another man. Okay, we were even, but then, why have children and make them suffer all the consequences? Oh how I wished that Vito were honest with me, and just tell me that he did not love me. Instead he would just say that I was crazy, that I was just making up problems. Indeed, I myself often wondered whether or not I was crazy.

Life was the same every day, work and home. We rarely went out, and I felt totally detached from Vito. I did not care about him anymore. Several times I tried to make contact with Mrs. Rosalia using the password she had given me, and I would actually see her and speak to her. But nothing changed. I resigned myself to the idea that my marriage was truly over. I felt so sorry for the children. Between their grandparents and their father, they had no peace. They could not even play in peace.

Everything the kids did seemed to annoy Vito. Whenever their grandparents went to their daughter's house, and I was alone with my children, it was so wonderful! We would go to the park, and I would play with them and talk to them. I always told them that their father loved them, but he had a bad temper.

Rocco was still very young and felt the commotion around him. Perhaps because of that or because I went to work and left him all day, at night when I put him to bed, he would not let me go. I had to sing some lullabies for him until he went to sleep. One evening Rocco was more restless than usual, so it took me longer to put him to sleep. My in-laws began to yell, saying that I was a terrible mother, and that I did not know how to educate my children. Then my father-in-law stood up as if to hit Rocco. The baby, scared by their screaming, began to cry louder as his grandpa moved closer toward him. At that point I stood in front of the crib and screamed, "You better stop! You have no right to touch my child!"

Then, I told my in-laws that I was tired of them and that I could not stand them any longer, screaming to emphasize my point. I was really tired. Every day they would complain to Vito about the kids' behavior. I just could not take it any longer.

That same night, they packed their suitcases and went to Giovanna's house. I was so relieved, until I discovered that mother-in-law told Vito that I had thrown them out of the house. He didn't speak to me anymore, and I was no longer allowed to see his parents. Vito continued to visit his parents alone and, whenever he came back from their house, he told me that they hated me and did not want to see me anymore. I did not mind. I did not care to see them either.

The animosity lasted for about a month. Then one day my brother-in-law, Stephen, came over to tell me that he wanted peace in our family. He invited me to come with Vito to his house. I did not really want to go, but I agreed anyway. Stephen had always cared about me and taken my side, when I needed him. Together with Vito and the kids, I went to Giovanna's house.

As soon as I went inside the house, I approached my father-in-law to greet him with the customary kiss on the cheek. He not only backed away from me, but also began to insult me. My mother-in-law quickly joined in. In my defense, I began to unleash all the bitterness I had inside.

But Vito did not let me finish. He started hitting me. I decided to take the kids and leave, but as soon as I got to the stairs I felt someone grabbing my hair and pulling me backwards. I turned around and caught a glimpse of Giovanna. She was upset about the harsh way I spoke to her parents. I fell down the stairs with Rocco in my arms. All three kids were crying. Badly shaken up they were yelling, "Let's go, Mama, let's go!" I hardly had the energy to get up, but I did, and I went looking for a taxi. Stephen, who had first tried to stop me, began to comfort me. He brought the boys and me home. On the way home he told me he was sorry about the ways things had turned out.

That night Vito spent the night at Giovanna's house, and I cried my heart out. I couldn't take it any longer. I needed somebody to talk to. Somebody I could trust. I kept thinking how stupid my life was, how I should leave Vito and put an end to my absurd life. Indeed, it was time to accept the end of my marriage.

I called my brother Stefano, and I told him what was going on. I cried so much on the phone that I could not even explain things well. My brother quickly understood and said, "Tomorrow morning, you'll go buy tickets for yourself and the kids and come back to Palermo." I promised him that I would do just that. A couple of minutes later my sister Aurora called me and made me promise the same thing. Finally, my father called and said the exact same thing. My head was spinning around but I started packing again, crying as I loaded the suitcases. At the same time I wishing I were dead. It was a night that I will never forget.

The next morning I called the travel agency. When Vito came home, I told him that I was leaving him, and that I needed the money for the tickets. He did not say a word, but went to the bank to get the money, giving me more than I needed. He was totally indifferent to my leaving him. Then I got dressed in black, like an old Sicilian widow and said, "As far as I am concerned you are indeed dead." Then I called a taxi and I left, without saying good-bye to him or anyone else.

The plane ride was hellish. The kids were very upset about our drastic departure, but they eventually fell asleep which gave me a little time to think. I reflected on the last years of my life, on my fate, on everything that had happened the days and weeks before my departure. I was so miserable that I prayed for the plane to crash. Everybody seemed to be staring at me, as if feeling pity. I had dark circles around my swollen eyes, a bruised lip, and a bald spot in my hair, where Giovanna had pulled my hair out. I must have looked scary, and I understood why people were staring at me.

After the eight-hour flight, I arrived in my beloved Palermo. It was one of those incredible spring days, when Mother Nature wants to remind us of how beautiful everything is here on earth. The sky was so blue and brilliant. The mountains around Palermo so luscious and green. It was April 26, 1976. I was thirty years old.

Everybody was waiting for me at the airport. They were very anxious to see me, more than any other time before. Papa was there, as always, and he ran toward me with his arms open. Mama started weeping as soon as she saw me. She really felt sorry for me. In fact, everybody was crying as if at a funeral.

Papa told me not to worry, that he would take good care of me and my children. I thanked him with my biggest hug ever, which came from the depth of my heart. My whole family tried to console me and promised to take care of me and my children. Papa even gave me his place in bed, so that I could again share the bed with Mama. He slept on the couch.

My parents were already taking care of Luigi's wife and two children, because Luigi was in jail. So the house was very crowded. Papa worked hard to care for us all, even though he should have been retired at his age. He worked hard, as if he were still a young man. There were nine of us in the house, but we were lacking nothing at all. He made sure that we had all the necessities. At night, when he came home from work, the kids would argue about who was going to hug him first. And when he went to work outside Palermo, just as he had done when I was a girl, he would bring the kids ice cream at night.

Mama and Papa were poor, but they were very generous. Whatever they had, they shared with all their hearts. Sometimes, I felt so sorry for us all. I would go to my room and cry, but Papa would come in and talk to me and comfort me. He knew I was very miserable. All my brothers and sisters also were taking their part in trying to make me feel better. Aurora came to see me every day and tried to spend time with me. She always brought something for the kids. Often enough, Mama would cook for everybody. Sometimes there was such confusion, but a happy confusion!

I finally made peace with myself in Palermo. I trusted my family and knew nobody would hurt me or my children. My cousin Romina also spent a lot of time with me. She was happily married and had two children, a boy and a girl. Romina could not believe the stories I was telling her. "How could Vito have changed that much?," she kept asking. We would also remember our happy childhood together, our summer in Capaci, and we would laugh together.

About two months after I had moved to Palermo, Vito began calling and saying that he wanted to talk to the children. Rocco would cry whenever he heard Vito's voice. Santino talked to him with a grown-up voice, as if to show that he was the man in the family now. Fabio would refuse to speak to him. Sometimes Santino would start crying and say, "Mama, Papa loves you, and he loves us too!" I did not know how to answer, especially when Rocco cried that he wanted his daddy back. Only Fabio seemed totally indifferent and seldom talked about Vito.

Vito started to call every day, but I hated it. I did not want to speak to him. I was so resentful and did not want to hear anything from him. Why was he being so affectionate toward the kids, anyway? And why was he trying to impress us in Palermo, while he abused us so much in New York?

One day, Vito called and told Santino that he was coming to get us and bring us back to New York. He asked Santino to tell me, since I refused to talk to him. Oh, how I really did not want him to come and spoil my peace! A couple of days later, he called again requesting to speak to me. I refused again, so he told Santino he was coming to Palermo the following day.

The kids were so happy, but I was very worried. I did not want to see him for fear that I would give in to his request of going back to him. I did not want to reopen the wound and suffer again. I went to the bedroom to think, and I cried. I heard the kids talking amongst themselves, overjoyed that their papa was finally coming to see them. Oh my God, what was I supposed to do? How could I feel comfortable with that man who had put me through so much pain?

Santino came looking for me, and he said, "Mama, Papa loves you. He told me to tell you that he loves you!" I didn't say anything, but Santino continued, "You know, Mama, when we were in America, I heard Papa tell his father, 'Don't stick your nose in my business! She is my wife!'" Then Santino hugged me and happily went to play. Those words came down into my heart, like a soothing lotion, and I remembered my promises to God. That same night there was a family reunion, and my whole family decided that the following day Vito would be put to the test. My brothers told me not to worry, that they would take care of everything.

I went out onto the terrace and sat there. I was sad, but anxious as well. I looked at the yard, and it was so beautiful, full of flowers in bloom. The jasmine had grown into a full tree and was now reaching into Bruno's balcony. Oh how beautiful it would be to return to those days, to go back in time and relive those innocent moments. I closed my eyes, and for a moment I could hear Bruno, playing his guitar, and singing our song, with his wonderful voice.

Oh, I wished to be back with Bruno! So many beautiful moments came to my mind. I wondered what kind of husband and father Bruno was. A while back, my aunt had told me a little more about Bruno. He had not been happily married either, and was now divorced. I had been shocked to hear that. In my heart, I had always thought of him as a happily married man, although in my dreams he had always been sick and calling my name. My aunt's words hurt me because I had hoped that at least Bruno was happy. Our fates had been cruel to us both, and we had suffered the same destiny. I had even prayed for him, so that his situation could be resolved.

When I opened my eyes, I looked really hard to see him, and there he was! I began to tremble and tried to approach him. Then I realized that it was his younger brother, who looked so much like Bruno. I was so taken by that quasi vision that I did not hear Mama calling me. I turned around and saw her staring at me in silence, as if she knew what I was doing there. I rushed into her arms, crying, and she hugged me and held me tight, like a baby. It was so good to feel the warmth of those soothing arms.

"Mama, Mama," I said, "Why did it have to end like this? I tried so much and prayed so much to have a happy family and a loving husband. I loved Vito with all my heart, and I don't understand why my marriage has ended." Mama tried to console me with her sweet words, and she told me not to worry about Vito's imminent arrival. I could always count on her support, regardless of the outcome of my meeting with Vito. I hugged her lovingly, and we went to bed.

Chapter 10
A New Attempt

The day of Vito's arrival I was very nervous. I didn't even know how to feel, whether happy or sad. My father and all of my brothers were with me, and the kids were so excited that I could hardly keep them still. Vito arrived in Palermo, but he went straight to his parents' house. That afternoon Rosetta's husband came to my Mama's house and said that Vito wanted to see me and the boys. I told him that he knew where to find us. Then, my father told him that before he allowed me to see Vito, he and my brothers would need to talk to him. My father, brothers, and brothers-in-law went to see him, while I stayed at home with the kids.

I waited nervously, and then one of my brothers came to get the kids to bring them to their father. I had been waiting for two hours, and I was a wreck. Finally, they all returned except Vito, who stayed at his parents' house. Papa said, "We spoke for a long time, and Vito is very sorry for all that he did to you. He wants another chance. He said that he will behave better with you and the kids, and he seems sincere to me."

"His promises are empty!" I shouted, "I don't want to go back to him!" Papa answered: "He sounds sincere, and you must also take your three children into consideration. They need a father! Try one more time, and if it doesn't work, you can come back here for good, you have my word." My brothers told me the same. Finally, I agreed to see him alone.

After three months of separation here we were, face to face again. We spoke for the longest time and for the first time ever in our married life, we expressed how we felt. Vito cried and said that he was really sorry. He asked me for for-giveness, and told me that he loved me. Hearing those words, my heart melted. I believed him, and I agreed to give him another chance.

The kids stayed at my parents' house, and I spent the night with Vito. For the first time since our honeymoon, he was very passionate. He showered me with kisses, hugs, and promises. During the few days that followed, we were like two kids in love for the first time again. We looked forward to being alone, and could not get enough of each other. He was so good to the kids too. He took them out every day and spent quality time with them, something he had never done before. All my resentment towards him vanished away.

My whole family was happy about our reconciliation. Rocco kept clinging to him, and calling him "my big daddy." Fabio was spending time with him, but still seemed to prefer my company. Santino was the happiest of all. He told me right away, "See, Mama, I told you that Papa loved you!" My family was happy to see me happy, and they all must have thought, "Finally, everything is okay!"

The last week in Palermo was amazing. Everything seemed so different, so happy, even the city itself looked pret-tier than I ever remembered. I wished so much we could stay and settle with this newly found peace, but we still did not have enough money to settle there. And so we had to go back. Sometimes ugly thoughts would come to my mind, but I chased them away. I really believed this time things would work out as I had dreamed.

After so many months in Sicily, it was really hard to leave Mama and Papa. I was now stronger but when it was time to say good-bye, I cried my heart out. I could not let go of their hugs. Looking back, before boarding the plane, I saw Papa again waving his hand towards me. Again, I said good-bye to my Palermo.

While in Palermo I had visited Mrs. Rosalia again and asked for her advice. She had told me that she was doing her best to get me back with my husband and promised she would always help. Now I was really starting to believe her. After three months in Palermo, I was returning to New York full of hope with my heart full of joy.

Vito was a true loving husband for a while. There were no fights, no arguments, nothing of the life before. Then my in-laws decided to move back with us. They came in and greeted me as if nothing had ever happened. I had told Vito that I did not want them in our house, and he had reassured me that they were going to live with their daughter. But now here they were, back on my doorstep. What could I do? I looked at Vito, and he knew my frustration, but said nothing to his parents.

The months that followed were rather calm. Vito was going out very little and spending more time with me and the kids. The days were good, and were passing by fast, especially after I began to work again. After living with us for two years, my in-laws, finally went back to Sicily, and I was truly happy to see them go. Finally, I had my house for my family, and my privacy. Nobody to constantly look over my shoulders.

After his parents' departure, Vito began talking about going back to Italy. Strangely, I was not happy about it. It was not that I did not want to go back. I would have been there in a short moment, but I was very scared, so I tried to get Vito to change his mind. We had tried going back before, and we had failed. Somehow, I knew we would fail again. Vito's parents encouraged him to try to settle in Sicily, but one day Vito said to me, "I think you are right. It would be too difficult. Besides, every time I go to Palermo, I can't wait to get back to New York." I was relieved, and for a while we did not talk about it.

The children were growing quickly. Santino was already in fourth grade and Fabio in second grade, Rocco was in kindergarten. It was easier for me to go to work, and I did my best to save as much money as possible. The occasion to spend our savings came when the house where we lived was put up for sale. Our landlord was very nice to us and asked us to buy it at a very good price. It was a rather small house, but we decided to buy it anyway. It suited our price range, and we thought we could move to a bigger house later on in life. We were very happy and started the paperwork.

Vito was happy until he called his parents who tried to dissuade him from his plan. My parents were very happy for us and congratulated us. Mama truly wanted us to return to Sicily for good, but she and Papa had resigned themselves to the idea of my living in America. All they wanted to know was that we were happy together.

A couple of weeks later, Vito's parents called him with some good news. They were very happy because they had found Vito a good job in Palermo. Vito was excited too. A few days later, he had everything ready for his departure. I convinced Vito to check out the story. The following week, he left for Palermo to find more about the job and to decide whether or not he would take it. I would stay with the kids in New York until he made a decision.

I kept working. With Mrs. Marta's help, I managed the household and took care of children. My neighbor was an angel. She helped me not just with the kids, but with everything and kept me very good company. She said she would be sorry to see me go back to Sicily.

Meanwhile Vito was totally enthusiastic about this new job. He called to tell me to get everything ready. I would leave as soon as the kids were out of school. A frantic life started for me. I had to sell the furniture and ship to Italy whatever I wanted back in Palermo. The days went by so fast, that I hardly had time to think about what I was doing.

As I was taking our first home apart, for the second time, I felt a sense of doom. I knew in my heart it would not work out, yet Vito was so happy!

One day Vito called to say that he had found a very nice house, not far from Aurora. She lived in the section of town called Giardini, a very beautiful place with lots of green plants and a natural water source. Oh, yes! I could be happy living next door to my sister! Now I was looking forward! As soon as school was out, I got everything ready. I decided to leave on the July 23, 1978. I had sold the furniture, shipped the luggage, and I was now ready. The only thing left was to say good-bye to Mrs. Marta. The moment was painful. We hugged, promising to write to each other.

Our arrival in Palermo was very festive. As usual Papa was the first one to greet me, but this time Vito was there too. He was so happy to see us! The kids ran toward him leaping and hugging him with such joy. He told me he could not wait to have me in his arms, but first he wanted to show me the house he had bought.

It was still under construction, but Vito described the design. Unfortunately, it was not the house he had described on the phone. It was not the one next door to my sister, but I did not say a thing. I did not want to spoil his happiness. I was happy too. The house would soon be ready, but for the time being we would live with my parents. So my parents moved out of their bedroom and added some cots in it so that all five of us had a place to sleep.

Vito loved his work. He was buying processed cheeses and selling them to local stores and supermarkets in the whole area. He had a set salary plus got a commission on anything he delivered.

Every weekend we would go watch our house, as it was being built. Every time we saw it, it looked nicer. It was situated in a new development, on the outskirts of Palermo, and there was such a beautiful view from it. I could see my beloved blue mountains and all sorts of vegetation, but most importantly, the house was right in the middle of an orange orchard. I could not ask for more. It was on one floor and had two bedrooms, a huge living/dining room, and a huge kitchen, a nice size bathroom, and a small room. It was also a very sunny house, which pleased me immensely. I already knew how I was going to furnish it, and I was truly happy.

In October, school started. It was hard for Santino and Fabio. They were supposed to be in fifth and third grades, but instead they were both put in classes with first graders. The principal said they had to learn the rudiments of written Italian before they would be passed to their regular grades. Rocco started first grade which was his right grade level, but he had the hardest time. He did not speak much Italian, and cried for a few days, unable to communicate with the other children. Santino was not happy to be with first graders. But every two months or so, they pushed him to the next grade. By the end of the year, he would finish at his right grade level. Fabio was the first one to adjust and did very well from the very beginning. Everything seemed to be working quite well for the boys.

Christmas was wonderful. After so many years, I was finally able to spend one at home with my whole family. It was such a special day! The house was small, but we were happy. Mama and Papa were also very happy to have us all around them, and my kids were totally enthusiastic about spending a Christmas with grandpa Aldo. My sisters and I cooked the most wonderful meal, giving Mama a break from cooking. It was a great and memorable day.

The day after Christmas, St. Stephen's Day, was also a holiday honoring the Christian martyr Stephen who was stoned for his beliefs. As I prepared to visit Vito's parents, I heard the doorbell ring so loud and continuously. "My God," I said, "the kids!" Mama opened the door, and a large crowd was standing across the street. A couple of very strong men were trying to lift a car. Under the car was Fabio! My heart stopped. My legs were failing me. I could not move! Thank God, Fabio was alive and crying, "Mama, Mama!" That cry gave me the strength to rush out to my baby. Fabio had blood coming out of his mouth and broken teeth.

We called Vito, who was already at his mother's house. My cousin, Tito, came over and drove us all to the hospital. Vito held Fabio, trying to comfort him as he cried hysterically. I sat next to them scared, but happy that Fabio was alive.

At the hospital they also found a broken hip, but he was alive! I thanked God for his mercy, and for watching over my child. Later that day, the neighbors told me what had happened. As Santino and Fabio were coming out of the house, a car going full speed had somehow skidded and landed on the sidewalk. Santino had tried to push his little brother out of the way, but had not been able to. The car had hit Fabio, leaving him trapped between the car and the wall. It was a real miracle that he had survived, and a real drama for Santino who felt guilty that he had not been able to push Fabio out of the way.

Fabio spent two months in the hospital for therapy. During that time, I discovered I was pregnant again. Vito was very happy, and so was I, except that I was now not feeling well. As during my other pregnancies, I was nauseous and vomited. Everything annoyed me. After Fabio came out of the hospital, he stayed at home for at least a month, during this time I stayed at home with him. He always wanted me next to him, and only Mama could take my place.

So many unforeseen things had happened in 1979, Fabio's accident and my pregnancy, I kept hoping everything would calm down. As spring approached, things appeared to be falling into place. The house was nearly finished, we had ordered all the new furniture, and the boys had adjusted very well in school.

Then I learned Vito was no longer happy with his job. He complained that his boss had not kept the promises, and his salary had gone down instead of increasing. Before long he started talking about moving back to New York, saying that the money he was making was not enough. "I am willing to go back to work," I pleaded, trying to discourage him. But he had made up his mind. Disappointed, I started packing our belongings to prepare to move again. Surprisingly, the boys were happy to be moving back to the States.

One morning as I was getting out of bed, I noticed that I was bleeding very heavily. I cried for Vito and Mama, and they ran to my side. They rushed me into the car and then into the hospital. As we drove, I was in so much pain, and continued to bleed. I arrived at the hospital a half hour later. But, it was too late. I had lost our baby. I cried so much, when the doctors told me. I was already three months pregnant and I had attached myself so strongly to the idea of having a baby girl.

That same day, my father had been sick. He had gone to Catania to watch a soccer match, and thought he had gotten sick on the fish that was served at the restaurant where he had lunch. While I was in the hospital after suffering a miscarriage, Papa was at home in bed.

The next day Aurora came to stay with me at the hospital. She had bad news. Papa was really sick. I began to cry and pray, "Oh, God, you have already taken my little creature, please don't take my Papa." The following day I was released. Aurora and Vito picked me up to take me home. As we pulled up, an ambulance was parked in front of Papa's house. Vito, Aurora, and I jumped out the car as fast as we could, just in time to say good-bye to Papa. When Papa saw me he said, "Get in bed, you should not be standing too long." He was smiling and seemed happy, but in my heart I knew that Papa would not come back home again.

That same day, Papa went into a coma. We were all

scared, especially Mama. We took turns staying with Papa in the hospital. Nobody slept. At home, we would sleep with our clothes on to be ready to leave at any moment. The doctors did a lot of blood tests, but Papa never recovered. After a few days, he miraculously woke up for a little while, but went back into a coma. For a few more days he continued to have periods of consciousness, but he would eventually slip back into a coma.

One day during one of his lucid moments, he told Mama, "Send Anna home. You know she is not feeling well." Poor Papa. His voice was so feeble, and he was so weak. Yet he continued to think us all. Seeing Papa with all those tubes coming out of him broke my heart. After a week, the doctors believed that he only had a couple of days to live. Determined, my brothers decided to make sure he had the opportunity to see Luigi, who was still in jail.

The following day Luigi was allowed to visit Papa. The hospital was full of police, and there were two policemen posted on each side of Papa's door too. No one was allowed to come or go. It was as if Luigi had been God-knows-what kind of killer! He was just a petty thief, but he received the most severe sentence because he repeated his crime.

When Luigi entered the room, he started crying. His blue eyes were red and his face was sad, full of remorse. We asked the policemen to remove his handcuffs, but they refused. So, with his hands cuffed behind his back, Luigi walked over to Papa's bed, lowered his head, kissed Papa on the forehead, and asked for his forgiveness. Papa was totally immobile, but his eyes filled with tears when he recognized Luigi's voice. Everybody in the room was crying, including the two policemen who brought in Luigi. A few minutes later the policemen took Luigi from the room. Luigi left crying like a baby, calling Papa's name over and over.

A few days later, Stefano and Angelo called from the hospital with good news. Papa had opened his eyes in the middle of the night and had began to talk! He had come out of the coma, and was looking better. They sounded very happy. Mama could not wait to get to the hospital and left immediately, while I waited for Aurora. At the hospital, we found Mama holding Papa hands; she said that he was sleeping. We looked at Papa, but he did not look like he was sleeping. He was all blue and cold. Aurora rang the emergency bell immediately.

Several doctors and nurses ran into his room at once, and took Papa to the intensive care unit. Aurora stayed to comfort Mama, while I ran to call Stefano and Angelo. As my brothers arrived at the hospital a doctor came out to tell us that there was not much that could be done for Papa. He would last one more day at the most.

Papa told us he wanted to die at home which was an ancient Sicilian custom. So we pressed the doctors, who were against it but finally agreed to our wishes. At 11:00 a.m. an ambulance brought Papa home. All the family, young and old, gathered around Papa's bed to say good-bye and to receive his final blessings. I knelt next to the bed and prayed. I asked God to let him die in peace without much suffering. At one o'clock a tear rolled down Papa's cheek. He died peacefully.

I will never forget that rainy, March day. The entire family was in so much pain. Mama was the most desperate, crying that she had no more reason to live and she too wanted to die with Papa. Words could not comfort her.

Mama and Papa had been married for forty-nine years. Papa had been for us all the best father of all. He was kind, loving, and always available when we needed his help. On March 31 Papa's funeral was held. Papa had known so many people. Even people from different towns came to pay their last respects.

Papa's death was a big loss. Papa was the person whom I loved the most. He had always been there for me. I tried not to cry in front of Mama, but when I was alone, I cried my heart out. I was very worried for Mama. She was so depressed. She was refusing to eat and was not sleeping.

A week after Papa's death, Vito left for New York. The children and I would join him when he found an apartment. I did not have the time nor strength to worry about Vito. I was so busy making mourning clothes for Mama and me. The house was always full of people coming and going, I had no time for myself whatsoever.

About a month later, Vito found an apartment and it was time to leave. It was a terrible separation, especially from Mama. She had gotten used to my being there to take care of her, and she was truly upset. When saying good-bye, I hugged her and tried to console her, but I wanted to yell out crying. At the airport I could not stop crying. When I looked back for my last good-bye, I almost saw Papa waving his hand to me. I had to remind myself that no, Papa was not there. He was dead.

All three of the kids were wonderful during the trip, perhaps because they knew that I was so sad. They were also happy to be returning to America to see their papa. Vito was anxiously waiting for us. He had rented a charming three bedroom apartment, which he had also furnished. He started to work again, still at night, and the kids were back in school. I stayed at home for a little while. I was depressed, but slowly I began to feel better. I called Mama very often. She was so depressed and crying all the time.

A couple of months later, I found a job working in a clothing factory. Vito was working at night, and I worked during the day. We saw each other very little, and slowly Vito started to go out with his friends again. I tried to talk with him, but he said that he was doing no harm. I was still in too much pain over the death of my father to even argue with him.

As time passed things got worse. Vito seldom came home. I was very sad and lonely. In this apartment, I did not have the comfort of Mrs. Marta, next door. I needed someone to talk to. Sometimes my girlfriend, Grazia, would come to visit me but not often, since she lived on the other side of town.

Toward the end of the year I suffered back and chest pain, but I didn't tell anyone. Vito never asked me about anything. I wished so much to have him close to me! He did not seem to realize that I was not eating, was constantly depressed, and losing weight.

One day in the factory while working, I felt very sick. My boss called the house and Vito came to get me. He drove me to a doctor who said there was nothing wrong with me. I was just stressed out. He prescribed some medications and encouraged me to stay at home for a few days. Just before Christmas, my in-laws came to New York. They spent five days with us and two days with Giovanna. During their visit my stress level became worse. My doctor changed my medication, but to no avail.

In March of 1980, my headaches became unbearable. I felt as if someone was pulling my brains out. The doctor persuaded me to go to the hospital to have a checkup. I left the boys with their grandparents, and I went to the hospital. Vito stayed with me a short while and left. As I sat alone in the waiting room of the hospital, I was overtaken by fear. Would I also die? It was the first anniversary of Papa's death.

At the hospital the doctors did all kinds of tests, but nothing was positive. They continued testing for a couple of days, but the test always came back negative. Meanwhile I felt terrible! On my third day in the hospital, I did not even have the strength to call the nurse. I had a very sharp pain in my chest, and could not lift my left arm. An incredible fear overtook me. I felt paralyzed.

At that same time my brother-in-law, Stephen, walked in. I waved at him to get the nurse. He pushed the emergency button, and the emergency staff came rushing into my room. There was such confusion around me! They said my heart was fine, and they put an oxygen mask on me. I was unable to speak, move, or even open my eyes. All I could do was think of my children, and what their lives would be like if I died. I thought about events of my life, and then I reasoned that it was better to die. I had suffered enough.

After a while I heard Vito come into my room. I did not hear Vito say anything, but I heard him cry. Then he took my hand and kissed it. He stayed next to me for a couple of hours.

The following day, I was feeling a little better but I still could not breath on my own. I remember Santino's face when he came to visit me. He clung to me crying. His sad expression gave me the strength to live. My kids needed me! I was on the respirator for three days. But after a week at the hospital, the doctor dismissed me, giving me a prescription for painkillers. The doctor assured me I would feel better soon.

The same day I arrived home, my in-laws went to live with Giovanna. Vito was rarely home. I passed out a couple of times and finally decided to stop taking all the medications. A friend from work came to visit me one day, and suggested that I visit a man who had solved her husband's health problems with massage therapy. I had nothing to lose.

That same night Vito and my co-worker's husband took me to a masseur. He started giving me massage therapy three times a week, and put me on a special diet. He told me that there was nothing wrong with me. Finally, I was really feeling better. I felt happy, serene. I even accepted Papa's death, and started to remember all those happy moments of my childhood. Papa had truly been a model father.

Chapter 11
Changes

Life went back to normal. I returned to my job at Fanelli Brothers, where I sewed vest pockets on men's suits. It wasn't exciting, but I liked the job because it was piece work and I was making pretty good money.

My daily routine was pretty simple. I took the kids to school in the morning. During the afternoons they were alone about an hour and a half. When I returned home, I prepared dinner for them and we spent time together. Santino was not doing well in school, but Fabio had very good grades. Rocco was not too crazy about going to school either.

All three of my boys were good looking. Rocco looked just like my Papa, and that made me very happy. Santino was fifteen and very interested in girls. The girls loved his eyes, which had changed from blue to green. Santino looked like Vito and my brother, Stefano, while Fabio looked like me.

In August Vito decided to go to Italy alone to close on the house we bought before returning to New York. He stayed for three weeks, completed all the paperwork and rented the house to my brother, Rino. At least we had solved the problem of what to do with the house.

To my surprise when Vito returned from Italy, he started talking about having another baby. "Another baby?" I thought. "We already have enough children!" I said opposing the idea. But eventually Vito got his wish, a month later I found out I was pregnant again.

In October, Vito and his friend, Bob, decided to go into business for themselves. They opened Italian Delights, a deli, in Brooklyn. It proved to be a good move for Vito. He was so happy, and I was even happier. Vito had always been such a hard worker. He deserved it!

Our family life suffered due to the demands of the deli. It was a huge establishment with about ten full-time employees. It required twenty-four-hour supervision. At night they made subs and sandwiches to deliver to stores and restaurants throughout the city. During the day, the deli was open for over-the-counter business. Vito went to work at four in the morning and came home at 11:00 a.m. He now had a real excuse not to be at home.

Vito was consumed with the deli. Every evening it took him at least two hours to close out the daily business and lock up. Sometimes, he never came home at all. I was nauseated with his behavior. We were arguing every day, and my suspicions were growing stronger.

My fifth pregnancy was the worst one. During my fifth month, my doctor ordered me to say in bed. I was constantly bleeding, especially when I stood up and I had stomach pains and nausea. How was I supposed to stay in bed with three young boys, a house to run, a husband, and a job I did not want to leave? As I pondered these thoughts I knew my job would have to go. Reluctantly I told my boss of my decision to quit.

Two months before my due date, Mama decided to come to visit me after Aurora called her and told her about my doctor's order. "Oh, my God!," I shouted. I was so delighted. It was her first time in America and it was such a comfort for me just knowing that she would be with me during my pregnancy. I was truly happy for the first time in a long time.

To my surprise Mama liked America. She found it rather quiet compared to Palermo, with its noisy street vendors. She enjoyed visiting the Statue of Liberty, and particularly liked the milk. She felt sad that Papa, who had always wanted to visit America, was not with her. Mama had to get used to shopping at supermarkets weekly, rather than buying groceries daily from street vendors. She also had to get used to the taste of the water, which she didn't like.

Mama grew angry watching Vito's behavior, but to keep peace, she never said anything to him. Two weeks before my delivery date, Vito announced that he was going to Atlantic City with some friends for the weekend. I was very opposed, but as usual my words fell on deaf ears. Mama supported me by reminding Vito of his responsibilities to his growing family, but it was useless. Vito left Friday afternoon and returned Sunday evening, as he had planned. During the whole weekend, he did not call home to see if everything was fine. When he came back, he looked happy and relaxed, but I had nearly worried myself to death. When I told him of my worries, he replied, "You'd think I had been gone for a month!" I was not in the mood to argue, so I let it go.

In the early morning hours of May 23, 1982, while I was getting out of bed, my water broke and I began to go into labor. Vito promised to return right away. Three hours passed, and my labor contractions were getting very close. Frantic, I started calling around town hoping to find him. I called the deli, but he was not there. I called the Italian Club, but he was not there either. Finally, I called Sarino, who immediately came over. While I was being helped into the car, Vito pulled up. He mumbled some excuses about why he was late. But I didn't want to hear it. I was so mad! How could he have left me for so long? Angry, I got in the car with Vito and Mama.

At three in the afternoon, after a difficult labor, I gave birth to another boy, Tony. He was healthy and so beautiful! You could easily pick him out from the group of babies in the nursery. I was happy that it was a boy, but Vito was disappointed. He wanted a girl. The boys were happy to have a baby brother. Little Tony brought a lot a joy to us all. Mama stayed with me, helping me along, and I thanked God for having her with me.

A week after Tony's birth, Vito told me that he was going to Atlantic City again for the weekend. "If you want to gamble, you could go for one night," I said trying to compromise. But Vito insisted on going for the whole weekend. Again he did not call home to find out how we were doing. It was absurd. Once again I started to suspect that his "friends" were probably nothing more than a "new girl friend." I never asked him, for fear that arguing would upset Mama. But Mama could see for herself that I was always alone.

Mama stayed with us for three months. When she left the boys and I were heartbroken. We had gotten used to having her around, always smiling and always giving. I was now truly depressed, as I tried to dedicate myself solely to my four children.

One day I told Vito that I was tired. Either he change his behavior or I would leave him. He started to treat me better. He went out less and every Wednesday night he took me to a restaurant. Fabio, who was thirteen, would usually baby-sit his little brothers, but sometimes I hired a baby-sitter. After about six weeks I realized that going out with Vito was totally useless. We would sit at the table completely silent. There was no conversation at all between us. He seemed completely bored with me. Finally I told him that if he was that bored with me, I preferred to stay at home. I guess he was just hoping to hear that, because we never went out for dinner on Wednesday nights again.

Meanwhile, Santino wanted to quit school. He was only fifteen and it was against the law. But I became worried when I found out he was going out with his friends, rather than going to school. Afraid that he might get in trouble, I went to his school to sign papers promising to accept responsibility for him. With my consent, Santino was allowed to drop out of school at fifteen.

Then I convinced Vito to take him to the deli as an apprentice, so at least he would learn a trade. He worked at the deli very happily, but sometimes he would come home upset and would not tell me why. Vito had forbidden me to go into the deli, and I did not understand that either. Deep down, I understood, but I did not want to accept it.

When Tony was a year old, we decided to sell the house in Sicily and buy one in New York. I was tired of living in a rented apartment. I had four children, and the landlord was always complaining that they were ruining his apartment. Finally, we bought a single-family home on Avenue F in Brooklyn. The house was nice with three bedrooms and a bathroom upstairs, and downstairs a large living room, a dining room, and a very nice kitchen. The basement was almost as big as another apartment. We finally had enough space around us. There was a small yard in front of the house, and a bigger one behind. I felt like I had a castle. I had a beautiful home, but I did not have my husband's love, the very thing I craved.

Meanwhile my sister Lisa had moved to the States with her family. Her husband, whose name was Diego, had arrived earlier. She and their three children had joined him. They didn't live too far from my house. Naturally, I was very happy to have my little sister nearby. I could vent and find comfort with Lisa.

A couple of months after my in-laws arrived, I heard a rumor that my husband had been seeing a 22-year-old Spanish girl named Blanca, who worked at the deli. It was war on the home front. Santino grew tired of hearing me argue with Vito, so he told me the truth. I was not crazy. They were really together. Vito introduced the girl to everyone at the deli as his girlfriend, and had even given her a ring.

Life at home was an inferno. Vito fired Santino, because he had insulted Blanca. So Bob, his partner, fired Blanca too. Of course, I knew that even if she did not work in the deli, they would still see each other. My husband was really crazy about Blanca, and at thirty-seven, I was no competition for a young woman.

One night motivated by intuition, I walked all the way to Blanca's house. I was sure Vito would be there. When I arrived I saw his car, and as I got closer, I noticed that he and Blanca were kissing. Vito was sitting in the car and Blanca was leaning into the window. I felt as if I had been struck in my heart. I will never forget that moment. As I stood there watching, Santino drove up in his car. His brakes squealed causing Vito and Blanca to look up. When they saw us, Vito pulled off and Blanca ran into her house, slamming the door.

I was so mad I could have gone after her and killed her, but Santino drove me home and tried to calm me down. That night Vito did not come home. Santino drove away in his car. I was worried about Santino, so I took a taxi to Blanca's house. As I suspected, Santino's car was there. I heard Santino arguing, and walked through the open door. As soon as Blanca saw me, she became scared. I asked her to tell me the truth, and she confessed that she loved Vito. "You can have him! I do not want him!" I hastily replied.

The following days were sad, as I tried to make some sense out of my life. The boys were sad too. My in-laws packed their bags and flew back to Italy.

For three months Vito slept at Sarino's house. Then one day he came to the house in a fury and tried to kick me out. Our sons sheltered me so he was unable to hit me, but he refused to leave, saying it was "his" house.

Vito moved into the basement, living there like a tenant. It was a really difficult situation. He only came home to sleep. He kept saying that I was crazy, and needed to go to a mental institution, arguing that he was tired of putting up with me. At one point I almost believed him. Maybe I really was crazy.

One night Vito did not home come at all. When he

returned the following night and found me washing clothes in the basement, he started fighting me. He hit me and threw anything at me that was in his reach. The kids were upstairs sleeping and could not hear my cries. Shaken by the pain of his blows and the mental anguish, I ran out of the house in my nightgown with no shoes on. I was running like crazy. When I saw a car coming my way, full speed, I thought of jumping in front of it. Then, the sweet faces of my children and of Mama entered my mind. I could hear them crying and calling my name. I stopped, and I cried my heart out.

Bitterness and hate flooded my heart. "Why do I have to put up with this man who has never respected me, and has always treated me like dirt?," I asked myself over and over again. I don't know how long I stayed there. Finally, when I had calmed, I walked back home. Vito was calmly sitting in a chair, but Santino, who had gone out looking for me, was very relieved to see me. He hugged me and walked me to my room.

Vito's affair lasted for about three and a half years. When the affair ended things finally calmed down a little. But there was nothing but a thick wall left between us. I tried to keep my marital vows. However, he did not appreciate me. Soon he began ignoring the boys and me again. Every now and then he would want to sleep with me. Although I would consent, I felt nothing for him. Sometimes he would become violent, pulling my hair and calling me bad words which made me feel cheap and dirty. When I was alone I cried.

My children were my only comfort. Santino had grown into a fine young man, and was going out with a very nice girl named Antonella. They had known each other since grade school, and I was really happy because I knew Antonella well too. Fabio was fifteen years old; Rocco, who was always very handsome, was twelve; and Tony, the baby, was growing up too. As Fabio had been, Tony was very attached to me, and followed me around. He had brown hair and eyes, a cute little nose, like his father's, and a beautiful smile. I was always at home with the boys, so we were very close.

I had finally gotten my drivers license, and once in a while, Vito let me drive his gold BMW. I was happy to just be able to go shopping or go out with the kids, even for a couple of hours. It was better than nothing.

Vito was traveling back and forth to Italy a lot. Sometimes he went just to see a soccer match or to visit his parents for the weekend. He just came and went as he pleased. He would tell me that he was going to Italy after he had purchased his ticket and wanted me to get his suitcase ready. Naturally we would always argue about his weekends in Italy. But my opposition fell upon deaf ears.

One day, while reading an Italian magazine, I read an advertisement about a book which caught my attention. The book was called La Magia Bianca, which means "white magic," and dealt with the occult. The ad claimed that the occult helped a lot of people solve their problems. I thought that it would be a good idea to have a personal copy and called the publisher to order one. I thought the book would help me get Vito's love back. Then, I would be happy.

Mrs. Rosalia had already died, and even if she had left me instructions on how to get in touch with her, I was too scared to do it. With this book I could help myself, without anybody's aid. I felt so happy. The key to my happiness would now be in my own hands.

When the book arrived, I sat down and read it in one day. I felt so empowered. All I had to do was practice its teachings. I learned how to read tarot cards. I had a new hobby, which seemed like a harmless game. I felt so strong. Nobody could hurt me any longer. I would be happy and I would help everybody with problems, especially women with marital problems. A new chapter of my life had started, I was gradually becoming a sorceress!

One night while sleeping, I felt very sharp pain in my whole body, particularly my back. It felt as if someone were torturing me. It was strange. I had never felt anything like it. I wanted to yell, but no sounds came out of my mouth. When I opened my eyes, I saw this terrible figure in front of me. It had the image of a devil, all red, with fiery red eyes and horns growing out of his head. He was laughing, and torturing me. I remembered the password to get in touch with Mrs. Rosalia, and softly said it. Mrs. Rosalia appeared and began fighting the devil. The devil disappeared.

Then Mrs. Rosalia stood in front of me and began forcing something into my mouth. She was holding a woman, who was a spirit, and was forcing her into my mouth. The woman spirit was yelling, as she entered me. I felt an unbearable pain. Mrs. Rosalia tried to put a baby spirit inside me, but it would not go down. Before disappearing she told me not to worry, no one could touch me now.

I awoke from the dream terrified. However, I remembered Mrs. Rosalia's final words which comforted me. A couple of nights later the same thing happened again. Now two people were inside of me. I was in pain. I felt as if my flesh was being cut to pieces, as if I were dying. Then Mrs. Rosalia repeated to me, "Now nobody can ever hurt you. Nobody can ever touch you." She also told me how old the two women were and what their names were.

It was a terrible experience, but from that night on I felt stronger. I began talking with the two women spirits that Mrs. Rosalia put in my mouth, and they began to guide me to what I should or should not do. I never saw them, but I could communicate with them. Then, little by little, I could also see a man, dressed in black with a black cape. I saw this figure everywhere. In the beginning, I was scared of him, but then we communicated freely. Then I was able to communicate with dead people. The first soul I contacted was that of my dear father. I was so happy to be able to communicate with him and have him always near me.

I also learned through my book how to come out of my body. I could see my body lying on the bed, while my spirit would go anywhere I wanted. I would often go to see Mama and make sure she was okay. I had entered into a tunnel of darkness, with no way out. If anybody hurt my feelings, I did not even have to want to avenge it; it would be done for me by the other spirits living inside of me. I was at their mercy, that is at the mercy of the devil, but I did not yet understand it. Actually, I felt powerful.

I started by helping some friends and relatives. If they needed help, I read their cards and helped them solve their problems. I spent all my free time with this obsession. Vito did not mind. Naturally, I wanted to read his cards and help him, but the spirit inside of me told me that I could help others, but not myself. Anyway, I could follow Vito, and I knew where he was at all times. When he came home, I told him exactly what he had done or where he had been. He would laugh at me.

I went to church every Sunday, but inside I felt guilty. My conscience told me I was doing something wrong, but I repeated to myself that I was helping others to ease my conscience.

In 1985 Mama, Aurora, and Emilio came to visit me from Italy. I was very happy that they were staying with me. Finally, I had my family with me again. They were with us for only two months, and while they were visiting, Vito, Tony and I went to Italy. Vito's sister Ella had a baby, who was going to be baptized, and my sister Aurora's daughter, Susanna, was being confirmed. We visited Italy for three weeks. I was to be Susanna sponsor into the Catholic Church. I had to go to confession and tried to explain to the priest about the occult practices. He asked me, "Are you hurting anyone?" I responded, "I only wanted to help people" and he gave me the absolution, his blessing. I felt relieved and forgiven, as if a huge load had been lifted off my heart. When I returned back to New York, I started practicing occult teachings again. Mama, Aurora, and Emilio, returned to Italy.

Everything was fine, except that Vito was still going out, and coming in late. I had not been able to make him fall in love with me again. We still lived in two different worlds, and he used me, but at least he was not hitting me anymore. First, because he was a little scared of my powers, and secondly because our boys were too big to allow him to touch me. I still held on to the hope that one day he would spend some time with me. For now, the time passed and the wall between us grew thicker.

The following year, Mama, Aurora, Emilio, and Susanna came to visit again. We were very happy to see each other again. I was in the good company of my family and did not worry much about Vito. We were so busy. Santino became engaged to Antonella, and we were planning a big engagement party for them. Antonella was a sweet and dear girl. And so beautiful! She would be the ideal wife for Santino, who was young and full of life. They thought of getting married in three or four years, because they were both so young. Mama was very happy to be able to celebrate Santino's engagement with us. She truly loved Antonella.

Mama, Aurora, and her family went back to Italy, after a few months. Around Christmas, Santino and Antonella set their wedding date for the following August. Vito and I were opposed, because they were so young. Antonella was only eighteen and Santino would be twenty in December. Although I talked to Santino about the responsibilities and difficulties of marriage, his mind was made up. So we started preparing for the wedding of our first son. I was full of joy and pride. I could not believe that time had passed so quickly. I still remembered my wedding preparations so well, and it was now Santino's turn.

The months seemed to fly by, as we planned for Santino's big day. The day before the wedding, Santino and I talked for a long time, hugging and crying as we talked. On August 20, 1988, at 10:00 a.m. Santino and Antonella exchanged marriage vows. Their wedding day was such a joyous occasion. Antonella wore a beautiful white gown embroidered with organza and pearls. Her veil, which I made, was twlece yards long with hearts and crystal stars hand stitched on it. Antonella looked lovely as she walked down the aisle with her bouquet of white roses. Santino wore a white tuxedo.

It was such an emotional time for me. I walked Santino to the altar, which was an Italian custom. At the reception we danced to a sweet song called "Mama." We cried so much, and I thanked God that He had given me the strength to see my son so happy. That was the first true present from life. My husband was happy too, and he also cried. Fabio was Santino's best man, while Rocco and Tony were escorts. For the happy occasion my in-laws, and several nephews and nieces flew in from Italy. After the wedding, the newlyweds left for Acapulco, the honeymoon trip that Vito and I gave them as a wedding present.

Life resumed as usual. I kept going out of my body to do occult work for other people. That kept me busy, especially at night, whenever Vito was out. Everyday I would communicate with Papa, and that made me feel safe and happy. However, I started to feel an emptiness in my heart. I tried to ignore it, but I couldn't. Every Sunday I would go to church, but my empty feelings were growing deeper. I thought perhaps it was because Santino did not live with me any longer or because Fabio and Rocco were growing up and going out at night.

Chapter 12
Jesus the Savior

A couple of months after Santino's wedding, I received a call from a friend, who said she wanted to send an Italian girl, named Marisa, to me. She wanted me to help Marisa solve her problems. When Marisa arrived we got acquainted and then I explained how I could help her. A week later she returned with her sister Paolina. Almost instantaneously we became friends. They were the first friends I had made in a long time. I felt comfortable with them from the very beginning. I was no longer afraid to make friends. They were both so dear. More and more we were felt as if we had known each other for a long time. Every day we spoke on the phone for a half hour, and occasionally we would visit with each other.

A couple of months after I met Marisa and Paolina, I invited them and their mother to pray with me. It was Good Friday, and I had decided to spend the whole day praying. After I had said the Rosary and prayed all my Catholic prayers, I found a Bible in my dresser, and I began to read it. My cousin had given me this Bible a few years earlier. I had tried to read it before, but after reading a couple of lines I always closed it and put it away because I did not understand it. This time, I was able to continue reading, and I understood what I read. From that day on, Marisa, Paolina, and I began reading and discussing the Bible, and the God whom we had thought to be too busy to worry about us.

One day one of Marisa's friends came to her house and spoke to her about Jesus. The following day, Marisa called me sounding very happy. With great enthusiasm she told me that she, her mother, and Paolina had all accepted Jesus into their heart. I spoke to them as if I understood what they were talking about, but I really did not. I felt I knew Jesus better than they did, however their happiness was contagious, and their words melted my heart.

Marisa was married and had a child about Tony's age. Her husband had separated from her the same day that her child was born. Paolina was happily married and had three children. They all lived in different apartments in the same building in Long Island.

One day they invited me to visit their homes, and to stay for a prayer meeting. They wanted to show me how they prayed. I was curious, and I asked Vito to take me and Tony to Long Island. When I arrived a woman, who was a prayer leader, started by singing a psalm. The words were, "Smile, Jesus loves you." As I listened to the words, I felt as if a dart struck into my heart. As I listened to that woman I fell in love with her prayers. She spoke of Jesus in such a sweet and realistic way, as if she was in love with Him. I was in shock.

Later that evening, Marisa drove me home. In the car, we continued to talk about Jesus. I thought I knew Him already, but I really did not. We got to my house very late, and Vito started fussing, accusing me of going out with Marisa behind his back. I was so offended by his accusations that I could not close my eyes all night. Then I remembered the words of the psalm that the woman had sang, and they gave me such comfort. They penetrated my heart and my mind and I started to cry. Finally, I got up and went into a different room. I was singing those words and crying myself to sleep.

When I got up the next morning, I had a beautiful inner peace and did not understand why. I did not understand what had happened to me. Marisa and Paolina had changed churches and were very happy about it. I kept telling myself, "I will never change churches!" But from that day on, my life changed. I kept postponing the occult jobs I had to do, and I never again touched the tarot cards. The two women inside of me were taking revenge in many different ways. I fell downstairs twice. And the man with the black cape kept reminding me of what I had to do. I started to be afraid of him. I saw him everywhere, he was always following me. At night, if I opened my eyes, he was sitting on the armchair next to my bed.

A few weeks later as I entered the deli, I saw my husband hugging a young Hispanic woman, who worked for him. It was nothing new for me, but this time I had enough. Vito and I started fighting again, but he repeated the usual story: I was crazy. I finally decided to leave him for good. What was the point of living with such a man? That night he did not come home.

The following day, I called Marisa and Paolina. They encouraged me to call Sister Marlina, the woman who led them in prayer. She would pray for me. I called her, and cried my heart out on the phone. She read Psalm 91 to me, which was medicine to my wounded heart. She then said that while we were praying, she had seen the Lord deliver me of all the evil spirits inside of me. I had never told her about what I did or that I had spirits inside of me.

From that day on, I began to pray with Sister Marlina and every day was like a miracle. I had a new found joy, I had never felt before. At home, the fights continued, but things were different. He could not take my peace from me. My desire to get to know Jesus grew stronger every day, and I decided that I would join an Evangelical church. Sister Marlina helped me find one. On July 2, 1989, for the first time in my life, I entered a non-Catholic church. It was the Evangel Church in Brooklyn, New York.

When I first went in, I sat on a pew in the last row, as if I were a spectator. The people were all singing and clapping their hands. At first I thought that they were all crazy. The pastor was speaking but, because of where I sat, I could not understand what he was saying. At one point I found myself raising my hand, and I did not even know why. Then I understood that the pastor wanted all the people who had raised their hand to come forward toward the altar. I arose and walked to the altar. Somebody prayed with me, and I accepted Jesus as my only Savior and Lord! It was July 1989.

When I went home, I was a different person. I felt free and happy. I renounced all the power of the occult. Later I burned all the occult material that I had in the house. After that, I did not even remember the names of the spirits that had lived inside of me. The Lord had sealed my heart, and I was now only listening to His words. It was as if I had closed a chapter of my life. I had fallen in love with Jesus. I was enthusiastically happy, and I cried and laughed with joy. Jesus had replaced my grief with joy. He had been merciful, and had given me salvation, and eternal life. Now I understood the gift that the angel wanted to give me so many years ago.

Vito was not happy about my "conversion," but did not say anything to stop me. He even drove me to the new church sometimes, because it was about a half-hour drive from our house. Tony always went with me. From then on, whenever anyone came to my house to find the "magical" cure of the occult, I would preach the word of God to them. The Lord helped me with the words and gave me a strength I had never experienced before. It is truly a blessing that most of the people who came in contact with me are now preaching the word of God too. I thought, "Isn't my Jesus great?"

I began to be more patient with Vito and to pray for him. I hoped with all my heart that Jesus would change him. I was still hurt about turmoil in my marriage, but now that I had met Jesus, I knew that someday He would save the whole family. With that promise in mind, I bore my suffering.

In April I found out that Santino and Antonella were expecting their first child, and that made me so happy. Vito was happy for Santino, but not too thrilled about the idea of becoming a grandfather. He did not want to be called grandpa. The other boys were happy that they would be uncles. On November 2, 1989, Antonella gave birth to the most beautiful baby girl, whom they named Anna, after me. She was so lovely, with pretty dark brown eyes and hair, and her grandfather's cute nose. Santino and Antonella, who were hoping for a girl, were very happy.

On November 5, 1989, a few days after becoming a "nanna," I was baptized. It was the most beautiful day for me. The baptism fulfilled a desire burning in my heart since the first day that I had met Jesus. I can truly say that it was the most beautiful day of my life. I was very emotional about it. Inside the water, I was talking and crying, but they were tears of joy which I had never before experienced. In that moment, I felt the presence of the Lord inside of me, and I raised my hands toward heaven and thanked Him. No one in my family went to church with me except little Tony, who always accompanied me. My baptism marked the beginning of new trials.

Vito had separated from me completely, rarely spending time with me. He continued with his trips to Italy for just two or three days: Roma, Milano, Palermo. He was spending money left and right, but whenever I asked him for a car, even a used one, he would say that he could not afford it. Yet he bought himself a new BMW. He was living the good life, dressed in Italian suits, with pockets full of cash. All of these things hurt me a lot, but I found the courage and strength in my faith. Only my Lord gave me the strength to endure.

At the end of 1990, my father-in-law became very sick. Although he had been sick before, this time it looked like he would not make it. Vito was summoned to return to Palermo. I begged him to take me with him. "I want to see Mama," I said. But I really wanted to go because the Lord had told me to speak to my father-in-law about salvation. I could not tell Vito, because he saw my religion as a sign of mental instability. Vito gave in and we left the boys with Antonella and Santino.

When we arrived in Palermo, we went straight to the hospital. I could hear a voice inside me telling me to act, but when I got inside my father-in-law's room and saw all the people around him, I felt nervous, as if I were surrounded by wolves. I could not utter a word. My father-in-law was sick, but able to speak. Although we were only scheduled to be in Palermo for ten days, two days before our departure Vito decided to extend the trip for another week. Despite the doctor's prognosis that there was nothing they could do, we stayed.

Every day the Lord told me the same thing, "Now it is the moment!" But I would say, "Forgive me God, but I cannot." My father-in-law did not have much time to live. As with Papa, he was allowed to die in his house, surrounded by his family.

The day my father-in-law was allowed to return home, I found the courage to talk to him. Although he was in a semi-coma, I asked Rosetta and her mother for permission to stand next to him to pray for him. Then I asked my husband to stay in the room with me, and I spoke to his father about Jesus. He nodded a couple of times, because he could not speak. I prayed for him and, at the end, I hugged and kissed a crying, dying old man. Even Vito cried, but did not say anything. Then, all at once, my father-in-law began to speak, calling family members by name. When we left, he hugged me, and I knew from the look on his face that he was asking for my forgiveness.

We flew back to Brooklyn hoping my father-in-law would continue to improve. But as soon as we arrived home, the phone rang. My brother-in-law called to inform us that my father-in-law had died. Vito and Sarino left immediately to go to the funeral. It was Thursday, January 25, 1990. The following Sunday, I went to church.

I was doubting that I had prayed well, but then I had a beautiful vision. I saw the Lord sitting on a throne dressed in a long white gown. Next to Him was my father-in-law, happily smiling. What happiness! My father-in-law had left in peace with the Lord. I recognized then the greatness of God's mercy. His goodness was great too and eternal. I could see that the Lord had prepared everything with care and love. I thanked Jesus for the great privilege that he had afforded me.

Chapter 13
Final Break Up

Shortly after my father-in-law's death, I began to suspect that Vito had yet a new girlfriend. We started fighting a lot, and I began to resent the Lord for not saving my husband. Gradually, I felt my peace crushing right under my feet.

Finally, I told Vito that it would better if he moved out. I packed his things, and put them by the door. I was firm in telling him that I did not want him in the house any longer. The house for him was like a hotel. He only came there to sleep, change his clothes, and sometimes to eat. I felt like a single mother, who was growing tired of doing it all. My mind was made up: Vito had to go! Realizing I was serious, he moved in with Giovanna, his sister.

I cried for a long time. I had hoped that my firmness would have caused Vito to stay and straighten up. I wanted him to understand that I wanted a real husband and a real father for my kids. He never understood that, and in all those years, he brought misery to our home. I wanted his love, but he despised me instead.

After three months, he decided to move back home. Prior to returning, Stephen stopped by to talk to me, and even the children asked me to give their father one more chance. Finally Vito came home, making all kinds of promises.

It was November 2, 1990, little Anna's first birthday. I warned Vito that I would not allow him to treat me like dirt. I would not allow him to openly talk about his relationships with other women, as he had gotten in the habit of doing never realizing how much he was hurting me.

From that day on, I prayed to find the strength to forgive Vito and to forget the past. Vito was going out very little, and when he went out, he came back early. I started to believe that perhaps, this was it. I could have my family together. But Vito resumed his old lifestyle. When he was home, everything had to be quiet. There was no talking or laughing. Everything seemed to annoy him. I tried to tolerate Vito's behavior. When I could not hold back my anger, there would be fights. On Wednesdays and Sundays, I would take a taxi to church, because it was too far to walk and Vito refused to buy me a car. Finally I decided I would work and buy my own car! So, I started sewing clothes from my basement again, to save enough money.

During the spring my mother-in-law came to visit us. She could not believe how much I had changed. I was more independent, more free. For the first time in my life, I felt like a real "person." Since I had met Jesus, I wanted to show everybody how happy He had made me. I welcomed her with open arms, trying my best to make her happy too. But she seemed to resent me, and complained to Vito whenever I went to church.

Although I was sewing from home, I would often baby-sit my granddaughter, Anna, while Antonella and Santino worked at the deli with Vito. Little Anna was adorable. Very beautiful, she looked like her grandfather in an astonishing way. Vito was fond of Anna, and happy that she looked like him. Rather than complaining when she called him "nonno," he seemed happy about it. Anna was a dear sweet child. I enjoyed watching her and making little dresses for her.

In September my mother-in-law went back to Italy. The Sunday before she left, I showed her a bouquet of roses that were lying on the seat of Vito's car, explaining that they were not for her or me. She looked at them, then turned to me and said, "You are right, Anna. My son does not behave well. Please have patience with him." I could not believe my ears!

For the first time in nearly twenty-five years she acknowledged Vito's behavior. I was so grateful.

When Anna turned two, Santino and Antonella decided to have a birthday party for her on Saturday, November 10. Vito had gone out in the afternoon, but returned for about an hour. He seemed to be in a hurry, and he kept asking Antonella to speed things up. About five minutes after Anna blew out the candles, he left. I was upset, but did not say anything because I did not want to spoil Anna's party.

Vito came home at 7:00 a.m. the next morning. From the moment he walked in the door, we argued. "This time it is really the end of our marriage," I yelled. As usual, his reply was that I was crazy. Since it was Sunday I started getting ready for church. When I returned home I began to straighten up. When I came across Vito's clothes, I noticed that his jacket was full of lipstick marks. As firmly as I could, I told him that I did not want to see him ever again. Vito gathered his things and left. Then I called his family in Palermo and told them that our marriage was over. I will never forget Sunday, November, 11 1991. It was the day Vito went completely out of my life.

I did not cry a bit after Vito left, but I felt as if a thorn had been taken out of my heart. After a week, Vito rented an apartment and bought new furniture. He took nothing from our home, but his "freedom." He was free of his wife and children. Free to enjoy his life as a bachelor.

A couple of weeks after our separation, Vito started sending me money every week by Santino or Fabio, who were both working with him. By January 1992, I had saved enough money to buy myself a car. I chose a 1983 Chevy Cavalier. I was so happy. I could now drive myself shopping or to church.

That same month Tony started having problems at school. He got into fights and was not studying at all. He was mad about the separation and showed his anger to the other kids.

I sought counsel from my pastor, who suggested that I enroll Tony in the Christian school operated by our church. It was expensive, but I decided to sacrifice everything to give Tony a better opportunity. God was helping me. Somehow I was able to buy a car, and I had found a good school for Tony.

After a few months, Vito started talking about getting back together with me. But I did not take him seriously. I had bouts of depression when I came to the realization that I had spent a lifetime just waiting for him to change. I had suffered, and our kids suffered. I had been so stupid taking so much abuse, always sensing that in the end I would be alone. I was going through an inner struggle trying to forgive him, but I could not.

Despite my ill feelings for Vito, I was still his wife. So I still wanted to know who he was seeing. I decided to hired a private investigator. My sons tried to stop me arguing it was "absurd, not worth my money!" But I insisted. After a month or so, the investigator brought me his report, which said Vito was dating a Mexican woman, and every time he went to see her, he would bring her red roses. He showed me pictures of Vito with her.

With the investigator's report in my hands, I called Vito over to the house. I showed him the pictures and report right in front of Santino. At first he turned as white as a dead man. Then he started denying the evidence. We argued for a while, but I had proven my point. I was not crazy after all. The following day I called a lawyer, and started divorce proceedings. It was February 1992, about twenty-five years from our wedding date.

When Vito found out I had taken money out of his bank account to pay the investigator he refused to send me any money, but he continued to pay the mortgage. I was really short on cash. I was using the money he gave me to pay Tony's tuition.

When I found it hard to make ends meet, I went into a nervous crisis. One day I went over to Vito's apartment and rang the doorbell. When he answered I started yelling at him. I felt like a bomb had just exploded inside of me. Angry, he closed the door in my face and would not allow me to come inside. I was out of my wits. I went down to his car, and started kicking and punching it. When Rocco drove up and saw me, he forced me into his car.

During the days that followed I was so sad I could not pray. I felt so guilty. In vain I had held on to the marriage for twenty-five years, not wanting to accept that it was doomed from the very beginning. By trying to hold the marriage together, I felt all I had done was ruin my life and my four kids. At night I could not sleep, and during the day I felt like a zombie. Thanks to the prayers of my sisters and brothers in the Lord, I began to feel better, but the crises were coming one after the other.

By the time summer arrived, I began to accept my situation. Life went on and I tried to live according to God's will. At times, I felt resentment toward God. I just could not understand why He had not changed Vito, especially since I had met Jesus. I was sure that Jesus would have changed my husband. I did not understand God's plan.

In the fall, I received a hymn from God, which I titled "I Praise You Lord." It was the first of many songs the Lord would give me and it filled me with such joy.

On November 2, 1992, little Anna turned three years old. Santino and Antonella invited Vito to attend her birthday party, which was being held at my house. At first I opposed the idea of Vito attending, but I changed my mind.

Vito arrived looking relaxed but was sort of detached. When it was time for the group picture, he stood next to me, smiling, as if nothing had ever happened. As soon as we were alone, he told me that he wanted to come back, but he still had some doubts. He wanted to know if I would give him a chance to date me again? I agreed to go out with him. I was having a lot of problems with Tony and wanted to talk to him. Of course, I was still hoping for that Vito would come to his senses. We set a date for the following week.

The days before our date, I started hoping for a miracle. After a year of separation, I felt there was hope that Vito might have changed. That Saturday night, I dressed so carefully wanting to look pretty for him. Vito picked me up on time and we went to La Boccaletta, an Italian restaurant in Queens. We discussed all the things that had happened over the years. Vito blamed me for the failure of our marriage. And of course, I argued that it was his fault.

He was not ready to come home. He said my new religion bothered him. I tried to explain how I felt about God. "God makes me love you even more," I explained. But Vito did not love me and he let me know. His words really hurt me, and while swallowing my tears, I asked, "Did you take me out just to tell me that? At least you could be honest with me for just once! I am tired of your lies." He answered, "You really want the truth? I'll give you the truth, then." But his version of the truth sounded more like another concocted story.

He said that last year he met a girl from Mexico that he was still seeing. He was trying to get rid of her, but according to her customs the only way he could be free of her was to find her a husband. He begged me to not say a word to anyone, or me and the kids would be in a danger. He claimed his life was always in danger because her brother had ties to the Mob and he carried a loaded gun. He acted as if he were afraid that somebody might see me with him and tell her!

I was speechless. He had really scared me. But, for some strange reason I believed him and even felt sorry for him. I told him that I would help by being patient and praying for him, although I was really scared for myself. We parted promising that we would call each other. That night I could not sleep, fearful for myself and my sons.

The following days were tense. I had promised Vito I would not to speak to anyone, so I didn't. Jesus was my only comfort, but the more I prayed, the more I realized that again Vito had abused my trust. He had made feel scared to go out, while he could go out with his girlfriend anytime he wanted. I was stuck, waiting for him to solve this mess. The following week I invited him for dinner. He said he would come, but he did not show up. For Fabio's birthday, I invited him again, but he did not even call. When I called him, he said that he had forgotten. After that, I never bothered to call him again.

Again he had put me aside like an old rag, and I was having a hard time dealing with it. I was going through an deep inner struggle again. Although I had started divorce proceedings, I really did not believe in divorce. I remembered my wedding vows to love him "until death do us part." But what could I do if he didn't want to be married to me? It was something that in all those years I had not been able to understand, or perhaps, I had not wanted to understand.

I spent my days in misery. Only my sisters in Christ could help me get through it. Jesus came to my rescue and led me by my hand like a little girl. He filled my heart with His great love. In the midst of my despair, I asked God to cause me to die, because I just couldn't take anymore. I fell asleep crying. Yet in my sleep, I saw the most glorious Jesus who spoke to me and comforted me. His words were sweet and His smile was radiant. His words pierced my mind. He said:

I am your Light
I am your Strength
I am your Peace
I am your Life
I am your Cover
I am your Joy

I am your Counselor
I am the one who brings you to Victory
I am your Husband.

When He had finished speaking, I leaned my head on His heart, and when I awoke it was morning. I felt happy and rested. I felt as if I had passed a test. Only Jesus' words and His smile counted. Even now, whenever I remember those words, I feel a great inner peace which helps me get along. I thank God for this great gift, and I tell everyone, all the suffering is worth it in view of what is waiting for us with Jesus.

Four months went by without a word from Vito. I decided to finally give up on our marriage and to put the pieces of my life back together. In Italy my family was really upset about what I was going through. Mama did not know much because she had a heart attack, and I did not want to upset her. Eventually, I had to tell her too, because whenever she called she always asked about Vito. The news of our separation was hard for her to take, but she still tried to comfort me.

In March 1993, Tony was sick with a very high fever. I rushed him to the hospital, where they put him in ice baths. All my older kids were with me to make sure their little brother would be okay. Thank God, it was not too serious, and that same night the doctors allowed Tony to come home. The next day, I heard a knock at the door. And to my surprise, it was Vito. He had come to see Tony. I let him in and while he went in Tony's room, I went into the kitchen. Then he joined me, and he said he needed to speak to me. "We have nothing to discuss," I said firmly.

We had a court date for our divorce hearing scheduled in May. Vito asked me to call the lawyer and stop the proceedings because he wanted to come back home to show me that he could keep his promise. I told him that I did not want to get hurt again. He promised that if he came, he would sleep in his own room until he was sure that he wanted to continue our marriage. I told him that I had to think about it, and I would call him.

When Vito left, I started praying. I even called some of my sisters in the Lord and asked them to pray for me. I was afraid of being hurt again, since my wound was somewhat healed. I prayed and prayed, until I was sure that I was making the right decision. When I finished I felt happy, because I believed that the Lord approved of my decision to take Vito back and was answering my prayers.

At the end of March, Vito moved back home. I fixed dinner and he sat there quietly, as we ate. It was like having a stranger in the house. But Tony was very happy to have both of his parents living under one roof again. Vito slept in Tony's room. He was also keeping his apartment until he was sure of what he wanted to do.

That night we slept in separate rooms. After going to bed, I heard him walk downstairs into the living room. Worried, I asked if he was feeling okay. I waited for a while and when he did not go back to bed, I asked him if I could join him. He answered that it would be fine.

I went downstairs and found Vito sitting on the couch with a bottle of whisky in his hand. He was drinking and looked really sad. I sat next to him, silently, and he began to talk. Under the effects of alcohol, he began to spill his guts out. He told me that he could not forget the other woman. Although he was in our home, his mind was with her. "My mind belongs to her," he said, "I cannot escape her, not even for a second."

He talked for hours. Each word was like a knife in my heart. Yet he begged me to help him. I could not utter a word. I prayed that Jesus would give me the courage to bear the pain. Vito stayed up talking until three in the morning. Then he began to cry. I walked him to his bedroom, but he was hysterical and told me to call Santino. He needed to go to the hospital. He looked like he was having problems breathing, so I ran down to the kitchen to call Santino, who lived a block down the street. "I'll be there in ten minutes," he said.

I went back upstairs to check on Vito. When I entered the room he was lying on the bed, and he looked dead. I shook him, but felt nothing. There were no signs of life, not even a pulse. I checked for his heart beat, but could not feel it. "Oh no, God, don't let him die now, not now!," I cried. I don't know how much time passed, but Vito opened his eyes and said, "Where am I?" At that moment Santino walked in. He was worried and tried to convince Vito to go to the hospital, but Vito refused.

I felt sorry for him, and I comforted him as if he were my child. He was very cold, so I put more blankets on him. When I saw how he was shaking, I laid next to him, and I hugged him. It was as if I were his mother. I stayed with him until he fell asleep. Then I went back to my bed, but I could not sleep for the rest of the night. The next morning he said that he had made up his mind. From now on he would sleep at his apartment.

Everyday, he came to my house to eat and change clothes, much like old times. My nerves were going to pieces, but I tried to stay calm. I knew the end result. Three weeks went by, and he spent one more night our home. Again he began drinking and talking about his girlfriend. When he looked like he was feeling sick again, and I moved next to him, he looked at me and said, "Don't you understand that you are repulsive?" I stood frozen. I left the room and went to bed. He also left, returning to his apartment. The following day he came to pick up his things. He claimed that moving in with me was an absurd idea. It would never work, because he loved his girlfriend too much.

From that day on, Vito never came back home or called again. I went back into a deep state of depression for the new wound that had opened in my heart. He had been cruel to me. After a year and a half, I had given him his last chance, and all he had done was talk to me about his love for his Mexican flame. I must have been really stupid to put up with that. There was nothing I could do, but forget about him once and for all. I cried for help from God.

For the first time since my marriage, I felt disgusted for struggling to keep my marriage intact at any cost. I was hurt because our sons had suffered so much pain and were still suffering. Santino, who was happily married, told me he was having nightmares about me and Vito fighting. Fabio was scared of serious commitment, and Rocco was so sad, he rarely spoke about his father. Tony was suffering too. Sometimes he would cry out for his daddy. Hurt because Vito was not there, Tony would get mad at me. He was always praying and hoping that his papa would come back. His tender age should have been the most beautiful and carefree time of his life, but he, too, was heartbroken.

As I reflected on all these things, I felt guilty about having idolized my marriage and I asked God for forgiveness. I thank God for opening my eyes, and allowing me to accept a divorce as His will. With the support of my sisters in the Lord, who prayed with me and for me, my children, especially Antonella, and my dearest friend, Tonia, I was ready to face life again.

Tonia was the mother of Tony's best friend, Michael. We first met when we moved to our house, but in the years after Vito left me, we became good friends. Tonia was discreet, sincere, and aside from Jesus, she was the one who inspired me to keep on going. Whenever I was depressed, Tonia cheered me up. She had the family I always dreamed of. Giuseppe, her husband, adored her, and her three boys were a pleasure. Tony was always welcome into Tonia's family, and they all loved him. Giuseppe loved Tony like his own son, and wherever he took Michael, he also took Tony. Tonia was a good cook, and sometimes she helped me sew. During these times we had time to confide in each other. My crisis was almost over, and the sun was finally shining again in my life.

Once I was free, I could go to church whenever I wanted to. So I went on Wednesdays to teach little girls, the Missionette. On weekends, I would often go to Long Island to visit my girlfriends, Marisa and Paolina. Whenever I had a difficult time, I would cry for help from Jesus. Sometimes, I would spend entire weeks without any sleep, but during the day, Tonia would be there to cheer me up.

One day during our usual chats, Tonia suggested that I take a vacation all by myself. I laughed. "Me, take a vacation alone? I had never even been able to buy a dress alone? I was scared at the thought of going anywhere alone." In May, however, my kids gave me a surprise. For Mother's Day, they gave me a seven-day cruise ticket! I insisted that I could not do it, but then I agreed and began making some clothes. I wanted to go to Italy, but since I had the money from the income tax return to use for that, I decided I would take two vacations, and go to Italy when I returned from the cruise. During my cruise Tony would stay with Santino and Antonella who would take him to Virginia to visit Antonella's sister. How was all of this happening? Was I really going on a vacation alone? I was happy, but I did share that with anyone.

Chapter 14
Vacation Time

As the day of my cruise drew near, Tonia helped me prepare by making new clothes. We made daytime and evening wear, all in bright sunny colors. I also had everything ready for my trip to Italy. Although I was excited about the cruise, I felt a little scared. What would I do all alone? I asked Tonia. She replied, "You'll see. You'll make friends!"

When the big day arrived Santino drove me to the port to board the *Royal Empress*. It was the July 11, 1993. I said good-bye to everyone, looking so happy. But inside, I felt like crying. An officer picked up my luggage and accompanied me to my cabin. Perhaps he noticed that I looked lost. When we began to talk he told me his name was Mario. He was from Brazil and worked in the dining room. When we reached my cabin he said good-bye, promising he would see me again.

My cabin was small, but comfortable. There was a little bed, a night table with a large mirror chest with drawers, two large closets, and a large bathroom. It was quite charming. I began to relax as I put my clothes away and got ready for dinner.

Everyone was assigned to a table. At my table, there was a young Russian woman with her children. We started talking her right away. As soon as Mario saw me, he came over to the table and invited me for a walk after dinner. My immediate reaction was to say no, but I accepted. What could be wrong with going for a walk? Mario brought me a red rose, and we walked around the deck. I was so silent. I had never taken a walk with a man other Vito, and I felt uneasy.

Mario did his best to make me feel comfortable. When we stopped and I looked him in the face, all I could see, was Vito's face. He talked like Vito and had his mannerism. Suddenly, I noticed that Mario was trying to kiss me. Annoyed, I told him that I was tired and wanted to return to my cabin. He looked disappointed, but smiling he said that he would see me the next day. He promised that he would make my vacation memorable. I agreed just to get rid of him, and I went straight to my cabin. As I prayed, the Lord helped me see that the devil was using Mario to try to tempt me. As usual, and Angel of the Lord had come to save my soul. I did not see Mario anymore.

I spent the next day reading and relaxing on the deck. I felt lonely and depressed, surrounded by strangers. I even started regretting that I had taken this vacation. At night I went to bed immediately after dinner. Thank God, the first day was over.

The next morning when I went into the dining hall for breakfast, I noticed a new man sitting at our table. He introduced himself to me. His name was Roger. He was a forty-nine-year-old single man from Canada. Roger seemed quite nice. He was tall with dark hair and had refined features. He soon was engaged in a conversation with the Russian lady. He explained that he had been cold at his table and had asked to be moved to another table. Roger remained part of our table party, and continued to keep making conversation during lunch as well.

That evening was the Captain's night. Everyone had to dress formally for dinner. So I put on my best dress, a short emerald green gown that made me look very elegant. As soon as Roger saw me, he told me I looked very beautiful. It sounded so strange to hear a man complimenting me! Roger was very considerate and kind. Before long, he pulled me into a conversation. We began to talk like old friends. We discussed our lives, families, and beliefs. I talked to him about Jesus, told him about my hymns, and all the miracles that God had done for me. We spent hours talking, and Roger was such a gentleman always listening and smiling.

When we arrived at Nassau, Bahamas, Roger and I were indivisible. We had such a good time, running along the beach, playing like children in the beautiful water of Nassau. The following day the ship stopped at Freeport, Bahamas, and we played on the beach again. I felt like a little girl, carefree and happy. Roger complimented me on everything, and for the first time in my life, I felt like a real woman. I came to realize that not all men were the same. There actually were men who were not after sex, and who could be kind, true friends. In Freeport, Roger and I spent the morning shopping. Later he told me if we lived closer, he would like to date me and perhaps it would develop into a more serious relationship.

Aside from the first two days, the cruise was a success. The ship was small, but very nice and the food was delicious. The beautiful sea was calm throughout the cruise, except for one day. Roger liked to take pictures of me, but we did not go dancing because Roger did not like to dance. We spent our evenings walking and talking. When the cruise was over, we exchanged phone numbers, promising to keep in touch. Roger wished me luck, and he said he hoped that someday I would meet the very nice man that I deserved. I thanked God that I had met him, for he had given me moments of carefree joy.

I came back from my vacation relaxed and tanned. My kids were happy to see me looking so happy. Santino was surprised when he saw me say good-bye to Roger at the port. But after I introduced him to Roger, he relaxed. Tonia was the happiest to see me. She had encouraged me to take this cruise and was thrilled that I had such a nice time.

I returned from the cruise on July 18. On the twenty-first I was scheduled to leave for Italy. Those few days at home were a little hectic, because I had so much to do unpacking and repacking. I wanted to leave things in order for Fabio and Rocco, even if Antonella was taking care of them. She would cook for them and wash their clothes. I would be back in September, just in time for school. And I was planning to enjoy this vacation at the beach, with Tony and the rest of my family. The day before I left, Roger called me to wish me a safe trip. He told me to have fun and not worry about anything.

When Tony and I left, we were so happy. When we arrived in Palermo, everyone was waiting to see us, especially Mama who had suffered two heart attacks. She looked so old and tiny. Poor Mama! They were all happy to see that I looked healthy and happy. My brother Stefano and his wife, Ninetta, offered to host us. I was so relieved I would not have to stay with Mama, who now lived next door to my mother-in-law. Since Vito left me, she had not bothered to call me. I did not want to see her.

Stefano and Ninetta had four children, three boys and a girl. Although they were teenagers, they seemed so grown up. They all made us feel very welcome, especially the kids who were all so affectionate. Their daughter, Dora, was the most charming and made me feel right at home. Tony was happy to have so many cousins around, who paid lots of attention to him.

As soon as I went to Mama's house, she insisted that I visit my mother-in-law. I did not want to, but I did just to make Mama happy. Mama had a good point. My mother-in-law, now was an old woman, still had the right to see her grandson. I called my mother-in-law, and when I said, "This is Anna," she replied "Anna who?" "How many Anna's do you know?," I asked. "Oh sorry, I did not recognize your voice. Where are you?," she asked. I told her that I was staying at my brother's house, and that I would bring Tony to her house for a visit.

When Tony and I went to her house, she seemed very cold and distant. I called Rosetta, and told her that I was at my brother's house. Surprised, she replied, "You know where I live, could you send Tony over?" I agreed and asked my nephew to take Tony to Rosetta's house, so she could meet him. During the remainder of my stay in Sicily, I did not see my in-laws again. I was rather happy. I had called them and paid my homage. I had been respectful and done Mama's will. I was at peace with myself.

Palermo seemed more beautiful than ever, perhaps, because with my newly found freedom. I was able to go out and do anything I wanted. When I had visited before with Vito, he always brought me to his mother's house, and left me there to rot. He went wherever he wanted, but I had to be quiet and obey his laws. This time, it was different. Stefano and Ninetta took me anyplace they went. Susanna, my niece, and I went to the beach every day. Everything was great, and the first week flew by.

Pretty soon thoughts of Bruno crept into my mind. I wanted to know what had happened to him since I had last seen him. Bruno's mother no longer lived next to Mama. No one knew much about the family, only that Bruno lived in France and had been divorced for a couple of years.

I decided to do some investigating, and I looked in the phone book. I found his brother Carlo's phone number, and decided to call. Carlo was surprised to hear from me, but he sounded happy and told me that his brother had been divorced for twelve years, and that he sometimes thought about me. He gave me Bruno's office phone number in France, and encouraged me to call him during office hours. Since I did not speak French, I asked Carlo if he thought Bruno would answer the phone. Carlo replied, "Oh, don't worry my sister-in-law will answer, and she speaks Italian.

I found it a little odd that Carlo mentioned a sister-in-law, and I was skeptical about calling. I thought perhaps Bruno had remarried. Curious, I called anyway. A woman did answer the phone. When I asked for Bruno she asked me who I was. "Anna Signori," I replied. When Bruno came to the telephone his reaction was really unexpected. He replied, "Anna, is it really you, or I am dreaming? Anna, you have no idea how happy I am to hear from you. All my life, I have been thinking about you and regretting that I ever left you." I could hear in his voice that he was moved, and I had no idea that I would caused such an emotional reaction. As he spoke, he cried.

Bruno went on to tell me that he had always loved me, and thought that I was happy living in America. He told me that his marriage had been a disaster, and that he had two children, Mario and Angelo. He said that he wanted to see me, and would come to Palermo as soon as he could take care of his business. He kept saying that he still did not believe that I had called him. Then, he asked for my phone number, so he could call me again.

When I hung up, I was shaking like a leaf. I cried and I laughed for no apparent reason. I thought that I was dreaming. I could not believe that Bruno had never forgotten me, just as I had never forgotten him. The fates had been so cruel to both of us.

The day after our long phone conversation, I was invited to lunch at my brother Rino's house. I waited for Bruno's phone call before I went there, but he did not call. I was concerned that he had changed his mind. Besides, who was the woman who had answered the phone? While I was at Rino's house, my brother told me that there was a call for me from a Mrs. Morano. "My God, what had I done? Was I getting in trouble because Bruno was married?" I went to the telephone with my heart in my throat.

To my surprise it was Bruno's mother. She sounded so

happy and affectionate. She told me that she had prayed all her life that Bruno and I would get back together. Bruno has suffered a lot, and had always been in love with me. The day before, when we spoke, he wrote down the wrong number, and he had called his mother to get in touch with me again. Mrs. Morano said that she lived not too far from Rino's house, so I promised that I would go and visit her. I was truly shaken, and Mama and brother were surprised. Rino offered to accompany me to Mrs. Morano's house.

When I arrived at the Morano house, I was received with open arms by Bruno's parents who were the most affectionate people. They told me that I looked very young and was still as beautiful as ever. While I was there the phone rang, and it was Bruno! Mrs. Morano announced excitedly, "Anna is here, you should see how beautiful she looks. She is more beautiful than when she was a young girl." Then I spoke to Bruno. His voice had not changed a bit. It was warm, soothing, and caressing to my ears. I had no idea of what was happening. It was all happening so very fast, but I was very happy. I began to dream again.

Carlo told me that he wanted to see me too. When he stopped by he said the same thing: Bruno had loved me all those years. In fact, Bruno was calling me every day, and we spent hours on the phone. He said that he was counting the days until his visit to Palermo. I once asked, "You haven't seen me in so long, what if I am fat?" He said sweetly, "It doesn't matter, I will love you anyway you are." I also began counting the days until his arrival. My sister, Aurora, and Mama were so happy for me.

Bruno was scheduled to come to Palermo on the eighth of August. He was driving from France to Italy. I told him that I was saving that day for him and that I would be at waiting at his mother's house. During his trip down to Sicily, he called me several times, always telling me how impatient he was to have me in his arms. In the afternoon Aurora and

Emilio took me to Mrs. Morano's house so I could wait for Bruno. He had told us that he would arrive around five, but he arrived at ten o'clock at night.

I was standing on the balcony when he arrived, and I almost fainted. I had to hold on to his mother's arm. He stared at me for a few seconds, and then he picked me up in his arms, and lifted me up in the air for what seemed to be a long time. We were both crying, and everyone was staring at us, but it did not matter. Bruno kept staring at me all night, and was always smiling. We could hardly talk the whole evening. I felt shy like a teenager, and I had the impression that this reunion was not really happening. I was sure I was dreaming it all.

When Bruno dropped me off at my brother's house, it was very late. He kissed me for the first time. His kiss was gentle and with such tenderness. Then he said, "Our love was so pure thirty-two years ago. We must keep it that way now too." I was so happy! I could not believe that Bruno and I were finally together, and that he had actually kissed me.

The following day, Bruno came to pick me up to show me his villa in Trappeto, a seaside resort area near Palermo. It was all so beautiful, completely surrounded by the country and sea. Many of the residents of Trappeto were very rich foreigners. We saw the villa, and then sat outside under a beautiful fruit tree to talk. It was incredible how we both had suffered the same kind of misfortunes and how life had separated us for thirty-two years. Bruno kept repeating that we had lost those years, and all for just a stupid misunderstanding. He said that he was afraid to wake up from the beautiful dream that he was now living.

Then, in the silence of that very beautiful place, he took my hands in his, looked me in the eyes, and said that he had a confession to make. He said that for many years he had been living with a woman whom he had met immediately after his divorce. He was lonely, he said, and she was there, but he had always mentioned me to her. He told me not to worry, that it was not a problem because they only had a platonic relationship. "Now that I have found you," he added, "I will never let you go again." I was disappointed, and I told him that I did not want to hurt anyone, but he gave me a hug and said, "Don't worry, everything will be fine."

Later that day, Bruno took me and his parents to Carlo's summer house. Carlo, his wife Roxanne, and their children had a very beautiful summer house in Capaci, the same small town where Mama had once sent me to forget Bruno, and in which beach I had written Bruno's name many times in the sand. Oh my God, this was so incredible! Was I really going there with him? Mr. and Mrs. Morano were very happy to see their son so relaxed and happily chatting with me. I was a little worried about the woman that Bruno had mentioned, but they reassured me, saying, "Don't worry. Elka is not a problem at all." We spent the best of times together.

The following day, Bruno and I went to pick up Tony, who was spending a couple of days with my cousin Romina and her family. Tony had fallen in love with Romina's house on the water, and had wanted to stay there, especially since Romina's husband had taken him fishing a couple of times, and her kids were entertaining him as well.

As soon as Tony saw Bruno, he asked me who he was. I told him that Bruno was a childhood friend. Bruno tried to befriend Tony from the very beginning and appeared to succeed. We decided to go to Segesta, a mountain that was home to an ancient Greek temple. I had not been there since my childhood, and I wanted to show the Greek temple to Tony. The place was always one of my favorite ancient history sites, with its magical temples surrounded by tropical plants and mountains.

When Tony saw Bruno holding my hand, he went into a jealousy fit, making our day miserable. I tried to explain to him that I knew Bruno before I knew his father, but to no avail. I begged Bruno to be patient with Tony, because he had been going through a very hard time during my separation. That night, I spoke with Tony for a long time.

Bruno came to get us every day. He drove a blue Mercedes Benz, and took us to the beach. Almost every night we ate at the Morano's house. After supper, Bruno would ask Tony where he wanted to go, and always consented to Tony's request. In the car, Tony would always sit up front in the passenger seat, and I sat on the back seat.

Bruno taught Tony how to swim and to dive into the water. Tony was having a great time. However, if Bruno so much as held my hand, Tony would go into rages of jealousy. Bruno did not mind. He told me that he loved me and Tony, and one day he would bring both of us to France with him.

Tony would not leave Bruno and I alone for one single moment. But then, unexpectedly, he decided he wanted to go stay at Romina's house for a while. The following days were absolutely wonderful. Bruno and I spent time all by ourselves. I will never be able to forget those days. Bruno was a kind, gentle man who would pay so much attention to each of my little wishes. I had never had so much attention in my whole life, and every little thing made me happy. We would hold each other's hands and look into each others eyes, like teenagers. Never in my life had I felt so wanted, so desired, so accepted for who I was. Both our families were astonished.

One day, Bruno knelt next to Mama and told her that all he wanted was to make me happy. He told my sons the same thing, when they called. He told Santino about our story and how much he loved me.

On the August 17, 1993, we went to a beautiful, isolated beach surrounded by cliffs that hang right into the water. It was just the two of us. Everything seemed still and silent around us, except for the waves breaking on the cliffs. Sloping gently down on one of the cliffs was a meadow, full of colorful wild flowers and palm trees. The ideal place for two people in love! Bruno and I were so overtaken by the beauty of that place that we fell on our knees and began to pray. We thanked God that he had given us the chance to meet again. Bruno kissed me gently, and we both swore to each other that we would never separate again. I thanked God that after so many years of suffering, He had now given me so much happiness.

That evening we went to Perla Del Golfo, a restaurant on the beach, and for the first time we danced together to the music of our old song. The restaurant was very crowded, but nobody existed but us. I was wearing a pretty, white, cotton dress, and Bruno wore white pants and a printed shirt. The whole day had been perfect.

Soon Bruno began making plans for our future. We would get married as soon as my divorce came final, and we would live in France. My sons would be free to stay in New York, or move to Paris with us. Bruno had his own business in Paris, where his sons and his brother also worked. He also agreed to help my sons find jobs. We spent a long time making plans, and Bruno kept telling me that I could plan everything just the way I liked it. He took me to his villa, still not quite finished, and told me that would be our summer house. I was free to furnish it as I liked. He then asked the architect to add one more bedroom to take care of the needs of such a large family.

The villa was one of four that his family owned in Altavilla Milicia, not too far from Palermo, in a sea resort area. The downstairs had a large living room, a dining room, a huge eat-in kitchen, and one bedroom. The upstairs had four large bedrooms, bathrooms and a large terrace overlooking the sea. Together with the rest of the family, Bruno was planning to build a common pool, that the four villas would share.

I was happy, and tried to enjoy this happiness every day,

fearing that it would vanish. Sometimes I would think about Elka, but Bruno would ensure me that he loved me. One day, while Bruno was hugging me, I started to cry telling him I was afraid we would never see each other again. Bruno told me to not think that way because he would never leave me. "This time", he said, "only death could keep us apart." I tried to believe him and enjoy the happiness of those precious days.

Chapter 15
Happiness and Reality Check

Every day we made plans. Everywhere we went, Bruno introduced me as his fiancee. He would tell everyone our story of lost love, and how I was his pride and joy. He never called me by my name, but always with a tender word, like love or joy. One day he told me that at one point in his life, he had lost his memory, and all he could remember of me were my blue eyes looking for his. I, on the other hand, could remember all the particulars of our relationship and tried to help him remember. He had the same deep green eyes that had pierced my heart at fifteen, the same deep voice. He had only gained a little weight over the years, and his hair was now white. His hands also seemed bigger. When I put my hand in his, my hand looked like a little girl's hand.

On Sunday, August 22, Bruno wanted to have a dinner party so that both our families could become reacquainted. It was a big party, with all my brothers and sisters and all their children. We had a very long, endless table in the garden, and while I was speaking to Mama, Emilio began to play the accordion. Bruno then gave me a diamond engagement ring! What a surprise! Nobody could believe how well he had organized the occasion. I was not the only one crying for joy. Then Bruno and I began to sing one of our old songs, accompanied by the accordion.

Everything was perfect, too perfect, and I was almost afraid of all this happiness which I had never before experienced. Bruno was making eye contact to reassure me. He would say that he truly understood my feelings because he felt the same way. He respected my feelings.

Tony was always unpredictable. One day he would be happy, the next day, he would hate everyone. He got along with Bruno, and even cared for him, but he would not admit it. Bruno did all he could to make Tony happy. Meanwhile, the time of our departure was slowly approaching. Tony and I were scheduled to leave on September seventh and Bruno was leaving on the sixth. I tried to enjoy the few days left, but deep in my heart I had a premonition that I would not see him again. Bruno understood it, and he would hold my hand tightly to reassure me that all would be fine.

Bruno's parents were the kindest of people, and his mother would introduce me to everyone as her future daughter-in-law. His father had the same mannerisms that Bruno had and even walked and talked like him. Whenever we were at home, he would say that he was truly overjoyed to see us happy and together, especially after what we both had gone through. He promised that he would make sure that our wedding would be big.

A week before our departure, Tony went to Romina's house for a few days. Romina was more beautiful than ever, and her happiness radiated around her. Enzo was a doting husband, and her two kids, already grown, an example of perfectly raised kids. She had been sorry about what had happened to me with Vito, and was happy now to see me back with Bruno.

When we went to pick up Tony up and to say good-bye to Romina, we found Tony playing on Romina's private beach with lots of kids around him. He looked really calm. He had been fishing almost every day with Enzo, and Romina told me how he would eat the fish as fast as she could cook them. Tony was not very happy to say good-bye to his Aunt Romina. He knew it would be the last good-bye before we left.

When we got in the car, Tony noticed the ring on my finger and went into a fit of rage. He would not speak for the rest of the day. We went to the beach, and he wasn't happy. We went to a restaurant, and he wouldn't eat. He was behaving like a monster, just to punish me. Bruno was not saying anything, but he looked sad. Finally, stressed out and sad because of the imminent departure, I started sobbing like a baby. I felt like an animal trapped in a cage, where there was no place for any happiness. Bruno tried to calm me down, but I could not calm myself. He stopped the car and went to buy a bottle of mineral water. When he came back, he sat in the back seat next to me and talked to me.

While we were engaged in our conversation, I did not realize that there was a man standing by the car window, asking Bruno if I were okay. He was Rosetta's son, Vito's nephew. I said that I was fine, and he said hello to Tony and left. When I realized the consequences of that encounter, I was devastated. I was sure that Vito would find out that I was somewhere in a car with Bruno, crying. That evening Tony got over his tantrums, and was again affectionate toward Bruno. He even pretended to be sleeping in the car, so that Bruno would carry him to bed. In his own way Tony loved Bruno.

On one of our last evenings together, we went to Mount Pellegrino, to the open-air Sicilian theater. It was a great show, but ended late and Tony was tired. Bruno carried him on his shoulders for the rest of the evening. They had so much fun together. Two days before the departure, Bruno took me to see the villa again to show me the changes that he had made. He insisted that I should be in charge of putting on the finishing touches. A knot came to my throat as I wondered if the dream would ever take place, the childhood dream which had now returned to me as a middle-aged woman. Bruno understood my thoughts, and he looked me in the eyes and said, "You will always be my little girl, and I will never leave you. This time, I will not let you get away!"

On our last evening together, Bruno asked Tony what he wanted to do. Tony said he wanted to go to the mountain for the last time, so we did. We drove up to San Martino delle Scale, as far up as was permitted. From the top of that beautiful, blue mountain, I could see the whole panorama of Palermo. It was so calm and silent. The only audible noise was the singing of the crickets. The sky was dark and full of stars, while the moon seemed to be smiling down on us. Tony fell asleep in the car, and Bruno and I hugged and prayed together, in what seemed a sacred shrine to our love.

September sixth arrived rather quickly, and Bruno was leaving that night. It was a sad day for both of us. I had a sharp pain in my heart due to my constant premonition that I would not see him again. He reassured me one more time that in Paris he would look for a bigger house, and clear everything up with Elka. He would let me know when I could reach him in France. I did not have to wait for the divorce. We could wait for the paperwork together. He promised that I could travel back and forth between New York and Paris as much as I wanted, so I could spend time with my older boys.

We spent the whole day in each other's arms sobbing. At one point, Bruno said, "Anna, remember that I have always loved you, that I love you, and that I will always love you. Regardless of what happens, I know that someday, even when we are old and walking with canes, we will be husband and wife."

He had decided to put his car on a ship to Naples and then continue driving all the way to Paris. I asked if I could go with him to the port, but he did not want me to accompany him, explaining that the separation would be harder that way.

I will never forget his red eyes, and sad expression when he said good-bye. He dried my tears with his hands, and then he kissed me and said that he needed to have a smile from me, to be able to remember it during his trip. We said good-bye one final time, wishing one another a safe trip. Then we parted. I stood in front of the house for a few minutes with my heart sad and broken.

I spent that evening at Mama's house because I needed her company. I would be leaving the following day. She was sad as always, but I told her to be happy because once I moved to France, we could see each other more often. My thoughts were on Bruno, who would be in Rome the following day, and I would be able to speak to him from the airport.

Tony and I left early in the morning, and when I arrived at the airport, the biggest surprise of my life was waiting for me. Vito's family was there! They were saying good-bye to Sarino and his family, who was returning to New York on the same flight as Tony and I. They totally ignored me and Tony.

From the airport in Rome, I called Bruno. He was so sweet and told me he would have called me again when I got home. During the flight, I did nothing but look at our pictures. The separation had been hard, but I had so much to look forward to! I thought back over all the events of the past months, and they all seemed like a dream. I had to keep on looking at my ring and at the pictures to believe that it had been true. Bruno had also told me that he was coming to New York in November, so I only had to wait two months before seeing him again.

When I got to New York, all my sons were waiting for me, and waiting to hear all the details. They were all so happy for me. They told me that my eyes were shining and radiating happiness. I could not stop telling them about my love story and how it all had worked out. They agreed that this was not a chance meeting, but a special encounter in agreement with God's plan.

Bruno was traveling for a few days, and was calling me

from his car phone from all over Europe. When he arrived at his house, he called me before entering. Together we prayed for Elka, because we did not want to hurt her. Bruno needed to talk to her as soon as possible, and he had to be honest with her.

The following morning, I called my lawyer and asked him to reopen my divorce proceeding, which he had stopped in March when Vito asked if he could come back home. To my surprise, the lawyer said that Vito's lawyer had already contacted him, requesting that he move ahead with the divorce. Vito had found out about my engagement to Bruno, and it wounded his pride. Therefore, he wanted to be the one to ask for the divorce.

Bruno called me daily, and in one of our conversations, he told me that during the last couple of nights in Palermo, he had the impression that a car was following him all the time. When I analyzed the situation, a feeling of nausea came over me. But more importantly, I wanted to know whether he had talked to Elka. When I asked, he said that he was sorry, but that he had not yet found the courage to do it. I told him that I understood, and I began to pray for Elka. I was sorry for her, but also concerned about my own well-being, and with the well-being of Bruno. We had both suffered so much pain, we now deserved some happiness.

A week after my arrival in New York, Bruno called me one day, in an alarmed state. He was very sad, and he just said, "My love, I need your help!" I did not know what to think. He then explained that he had talked to Elka, and she had left the house in a frenzy threatening to commit suicide. He had looked for her and could not find her. He cried out again: "Please, help me!"

I started shaking like an autumn leaf, and I felt so sorry for Elka. I prayed with Bruno that the angels of the Lord would help him locate her, and that she would return home safely. I reassured him that she would be okay, and tried to

168

convince him that it was not his fault. We had not wanted her to get hurt. He ended the conversation with the promise that he would let me know what had happened. About half an hour later, he called me to tell me that Elka was back.

Before Bruno had come to Palermo, he and Elka had bought tickets for a vacation in Turkey. And, they were still planning to go. I was hurt, but understood his promise to her. Besides what could I do? From Turkey, Bruno called me only once, to reassure me that all was going to happen according to our plan. He said that Elka never left him alone for a minute, and that he could not call me again. He would call his sister-in-law in Paris to give me news of him. Everyone tried to convince me that everything would be okay. His parents, his brothers, and his whole family kept telling me that his affair with Elka was not serious, and that he did not love her. They all reassured me that Bruno would marry me.

Meanwhile Vito told Santino that he wanted to see me. I was a little frightened, because I thought that he was going to give me a hard time about keeping custody of Tony. So I welcomed him calmly, without any intentions of arguing with him. My suspicions were right. Vito wanted to get custody of Tony. That was the only tactic he could use to hinder our divorce proceedings. I could see that I had wounded his pride.

He accused me of sleeping with Bruno, and said he was disappointed to see that I was behaving like a slut. I could not believe my ears! "What right do you have to tell me about sluts, since you left me for one," I yelled. "God knows the truth, and I do not want to see you ever again!," I added. I did not fear losing Tony because I was a good mother.

Vito also told me his mother had complained about not being able to see Tony. I told him I had taken Tony to see his mother. Tony, who was standing nearby, confirmed my words. Upset, Vito left, slamming the door behind him.

The anger that I had kept bottled up inside for twenty-five years emerged. How could he say such things? How could he accuse me of cheating on him, after he had repeatedly cheated on me. It was absurd. I tried to calm myself down. I had tried so hard to forgive and forget, and I was almost convinced that I had succeeded. But, I had not. I needed to pray to soothe my angered soul. I needed Jesus to give me His peace.

Bruno continued to call at least once a week, but he seemed less euphoric, and less anxious to talk. Then, one day, he confessed, "I am so sorry, Anna. For the time being, I am unable to leave Elka. She is taking it too hard, and I don't want to hurt her. I need more time than I thought. Remember that I love you." I felt sorry about Elka's suffering, but what about mine? I was suffering too! He knew how much I had gone through with Vito. Was it fair to put me through another hell? I tried to remain calm and to think positive thoughts. I wrote to him every day, but Bruno never wrote me back. He said that he did not like to write letters. He preferred to call, but his phone calls were becoming scarce. Oh, that premonition of mine!

About a month later Bruno, called me and told me that he honestly thought that it was over between us. He could not leave Elka. He had realized that their relationship was strong, and he wanted to give it a better chance. When I began crying, he said, "I am so sorry, I do not want to hurt you, but it is better to be honest. I will call you again." Then he added, "If your faith is so strong, you can hope for something, but I cannot promise you anything." I could not believe my ears. Was that really my Bruno speaking? The same Bruno who swore eternal love to me? If I had run away, would he have come looking for me?

I fell into a deep depression, thinking that I was not destined to enjoy any kind of happiness with a man. Bruno was a sincere and honest man. He had loved me, and wanted me. His love could have not been faked. His eyes, red because of tears, could have not been telling me a lie. I could not believe that he was telling me the truth now, and not before.

I decided to call Bruno's mother and ask her opinion. I was crying so hard, that I could hardly explain to her what had happened. Mrs. Morano was so kind and tried to comfort me. She told me to calm down, because Bruno loved me and not Elka. She reassured me that there was nothing serious between Bruno and Elka, and that Elka was probably just trying to keep him from leaving her. She told me to be patient and wait. "Things have a way of unscrambling themselves," she said. However, Bruno never called me again.

One day I received a letter from Mrs. Morano which really surprised me. The letter read:

Dearest Anna,

I am sorry that you think that Bruno loves Elka more than he loves you. If that were true, he would have not left France leaving his business half attended and driving for days, just to come here to see you. His relationship with Elka is already over. Just like we have told you before, between them it was never anything serious. She was for him very supportive when he needed someone, especially since he was also away from us all. Coming back to you, in Palermo, was for him going back to his dream lost thirty-two years ago. It was going back to his youth.

You never really had a chance to get to know my son's character. He is the kind of person who is very considerate about other people's feeling more than about his own feelings. I have not spoken with him, not too much, but I know that he is presently stressed out, and I never heard him so depressed. In my opinion the cause of this misunderstanding goes back to your son Tony. Bruno did a lot to ingratiate Tony, but Tony hates him. His fits were not just jealousy, but fits of hate. He even went to tell everything to his father, who is now trying to spoil everything for you. I have just received an anonymous call which told me to warn Bruno to forget your name. I have not told anything to Bruno yet.

Bruno is presently in therapy, and his therapist told him that his relationship with your son would never improve, but would get worse as Tony goes through his teenager years. My son has suffered a lot of hardships, and I imagine that he is suffering now as well.

He tells you that he does not want to leave Elka, but the truth is what I have just told you. His two sons adore him, and I think that he is not ready to deal with your son.

In Turkey he was very sick, that's why he did not call you. You know how suffering affects sensitive people. You know how much he loved you, and, believe me, my son has always been sincere. He thought that he had found the happiness which you denied him thirty-two years ago, because of your pride.

I am sorry to be telling you all of this, but it is the truth. I do not know at what price your husband is giving you the divorce, and I wish you all the luck for that, but he should do something with your son. Tony will never want to see you with another man. Please don't mention anything to Bruno, because he will always tell you that he is leaving you because he doesn't want to leave Elka. Doing that, he takes the whole responsibility of why his relationship with you has ended.

Anyway, I will be going to France soon, where I can see for myself how he is doing, and I will be able to give him the comfort he needs.

Sincerely,
Eva Morano

When I finished reading her letter, I was in shock. So Bruno was not leaving me because of Elka. I was sure, it was not Tony either. Tony just needed to be understood. It was obvious that a child would not want his father replaced. The only thing I could focus on was the phone call mentioned in the letter. I had feared something like that for a long time.

I called Mrs. Morano immediately. I was worried about Bruno's health. When I spoke with her, she said Bruno was sick. She also confirmed the phone call, and told me that she now was worried about Bruno. I asked her if Bruno knew about the phone calls, and she said that he had a pretty good idea. She also said that they feared for their safety and were going to France in a few days. We spoke for a couple of minutes, and she was as kind as ever. I did not ask what she meant in the letter when she wrote about the happiness which I had denied Bruno. Anyway, it did not matter now.

When I hung up, I cried out of rage, suspecting that Vito was behind the anonymous phone calls. "Why did he want to destroy my life? Why did he want to destroy the person who could make me happy? How could he frighten two older people who lived all by themselves? How could I forgive him?" I tossed these questions around in my mind, then I decided that I would not let him get away with it. I would fight back. I called Vito and told him to leave Bruno alone. "You can hurt me if he so pleased, but not Bruno!" Truly out of my wits, I began to threaten Vito.

The following day, I called Bruno. Now that I knew the truth, I felt I had the right to call him. I also wanted to know how he was doing. He was not there, but I kept trying until I was able to reach him. He said he was doing well. Naturally, as I promised his mother, I did not say anything about the phone calls he had received. I told him that I was ready to wait as long as he needed. Again, he said he was not giving me any hopes. I told him that I loved him and asked him to call me sometimes. He said he would and hung up.

Weeks went by, and I never heard from him. It seemed it had been all a great illusion. Hoping to find happiness had been an illusion. Everything seemed so far, so distant in time and space. I had only a little hope in my heart, because I loved Bruno so much. I could not help but think about him. I wrote to him every day. I sent poems written for him, and even two songs which I taped especially for him. I also sent him all the pictures which we had taken in the summer, but he never called, not even for Christmas. I called him, but he was not in the office. I called him on New Year's Day, left messages left and right, but he never returned any of them.

The first week of January, I called his office at 6:30 a.m., Paris time, trying to catch him before he started work, but his brother Federico answered the phone. He told me that Bruno was not there yet, and then he added: "Do you know that Bruno and Elka have separated for good? He is available now, don't let him get away!" I thanked him for the good news and I told him I loved him too. He laughed and told me he would give the message to Bruno and encourage him to call me. When I hung up the phone, I was so happy! With Elka out of Bruno's life, I knew things between us would be patched up.

The days went by and Bruno never called me. I kept fantasizing about him coming to New York, and could just see him standing in front of my house. I was happy. Sometimes, a scary thought would creep into my mind, but I would chase it away. Things would work out. Nobody could separate us.

On January 10, I received a letter from Bruno. It was his first letter ever, and I sensed it did not carry good news. When I opened the letter, my legs began to shake, and my heart felt as if it stopped. No, it could not be possible! Was I reading this, or was it just a bad dream? His letter was very clear. He wrote that our relationship was over. He told me that he had realized that his love for Elka was stronger than he thought. It was a very long letter full of strange sentences, such as: "I hope that God is great enough to give you some wisdom," or "After such a life of misery, you deserve better." A final sentence that struck me was: "I am a good Christian, and I have faith, but sometimes I lose my faith wondering why God who is so Great, allows such suffering in the world. Why do good people, like us, have to suffer so much?"

In those sentences I read that Bruno still loved me, but was forced to leave me. I knew that he was suffering for me, just like I was suffering for him. My poor love! I decided to call him and ask him exactly what he meant. I wanted to hear it from his mouth. Oh, had we been closer, I would have gone in person. On the phone he confirmed the letter. He told me that it was all in God's hands. God had allowed us to meet again after thirty-two years and He would allow us to meet again, if we were destined. Until then, it would be better to wait in silence. I wanted to cry out to him and tell him that I knew that he had left Elka, but instead I said, "Bruno, are you sure that you are telling me the truth?" And he replied: "My love, right this moment I would rather die than hurt you, so please accept the situation for what it is."

I hung the phone up, and I cried. I no longer knew what to think, but I knew that it was not Elka, nor Tony's fault. I didn't know what the truth was, and perhaps, I will never know. In my prayers I ask God to enlighten me someday, so that I will know what really happened.

Bruno is a very honest man, a good and sensitive man. He would never hurt a fly, and I am sure, with all my heart, that he was sincere with me when he told me that he loved me. The love that he had for me was as clear as ever. It was evident in all that he did for me, in his behavior and in his eyes. The month we spent together was compensation for a life of misery. I never thought that at my age, I could live a month of the purest and most passionate love. That love will remain with me for the rest of my life. It will help me live my life alone, warming my heart on cold winter nights.

Chapter 16
Light at the end of the Tunnel

I went through days of pure desperation and depression. I could not accept that my reunion with Bruno was over. Especially difficult was the fact that I had no idea why. I kept blaming Vito for everything. I was sure he had been up to something. I had experienced again that pure, romantic love, and I could not let go. I could not even imagine my life without Bruno, but there was nothing I could do. I had to go back to Jesus, the Prince of Peace, my only Comfort, He who in His love and great patience, pulled me out of this mess, and put me back on the path of peace.

I kept asking myself the same questions over and over. All I wanted was to love and to be loved. Why was it that I was always rejected and thrown away? When I had not expected love any longer, it came to me. When I expected love, it left me again. God had allowed me to enjoy that month with Bruno as if a dream to experience love fully, and I thanked the Lord for having given me that chance.

I finally submitted myself to God, and committed myself to live only for him. The Lord taught me that in this life there is no perfect love, and there was no such thing as perfect happiness. God had given me that month with Bruno just to make me realize that I was putting too much in the happiness with a man and not with Him. Only God is the author of perfect love, and he had waited for me with patience and care. He had prepared the year, the month, and the day of my encounter with him. He already knew long before I was born.

When I look back over my life, I realize that the Lord had

always been with me, giving me the patience and the strength I needed. I know that "in all things God works for the good of those who love him..." as written in Romans 8:28 (NIV), and just like King David says in Psalm 94:17-19, "Unless the Lord had given me help, I would soon have dwelt in silence of death. When I said, "My foot is slipping," your love, O Lord, supported me. When anxiety was great within me, your consolation brought joy to my soul." (NIV)

Two months went by, it was now March 1994. I had not yet forgotten Bruno. He was the most beautiful gift that God had given to me. I did not know what God had in store for me to help me meet him again. Perhaps, I would talk to Bruno about God, but I continued to pray that our paths would cross again.

My divorce was moving very slowly. Every now and then, Vito came by to pick up Tony, who was nearly twelve. Meanwhile, Fabio, who was twenty-four, had moved to Savannah, Georgia, and was working there. Rocco, who was twenty-one, was still living with me, but as usual he did not talk much.

In the month of April, Mama got really sick. I went back to Italy with my sister, Lisa, We traveled with our hearts in our throats, fearing we'd find her dead. Luckily, she improved as soon as we got there. The biggest news was that she too had also accepted Jesus into her heart, and that made me very happy.

Since the time that I had lived alone, I had made many friends. God helped me accept myself and to forgive myself of all my shortcomings. I still had to work on forgiving Vito, but it was not easy. I kept asking myself the same old question: "Why did he ever marry me?" So I decided to go to therapy.

One day, at a therapy session, the counselor asked: "Anna, what do you think? Do you think that your husband loves you?" I told him that I believed that somewhere deep in his heart Vito must have loved me. The godly man answered, "I hate to disappoint you, Anna, but I don't think that man has ever loved you. When a person loves, he does not want to hurt." I was disappointed to hear that, but when I reflected, I knew that he was right. Vito never loved me. I had just refused to accept it.

Slowly I learned not to be afraid of Vito nor to care about what he thought of me. I found a thick shield to protect myself from him. God had given it to me, and it protected me from everything. I also knew that God would save him too, and I waited with patience for that day.

By praying and releasing my pain, I slowly cleansed myself of my hate for Vito and his family. I only feel pity for all of them. I was sorry that he never realized how he destroyed his sons and I, who had loved him. His life was filled with women, alcohol, and gambling. I had forgiven myself, and him too, and I still hoped that he would change. My sons had not met Jesus yet, but I am sure that day will come for them as well. They are wonderful kids, and they love me very much.

In the winter of 1994 I had began visiting a Spanish-speaking church, near my house. The pastors, a husband and wife, were Hispanic. At first I was troubled because I hated everything Hispanic, but soon I learned to love all the members. It was a Salvation Army church. I joined and became a Soldier of Jesus, and even wore the blue Salvation Army uniform. I was singing in the choir every Sunday. I shared all the hymns that God had given me; on Wednesday I taught the children, and on Sunday, I taught Sunday School. I was happy to be serving the Lord, for His Glory, and I was thankful to pastor, Captain Miglia, his wife Lisa, and their seven children for giving me the chance to serve the Lord.

Tony was still attending the church school, and was followed closely by the teachers, and by the pastor. I was so thankful to them, especially to the pastor's wife, Mrs. Smith, who counseled Tony and helped him get over some of his anger.

In the fall, I began working at a local deli. I was tired of being home all by myself. I worked making and selling sandwiches, and it was sort of fun. I liked the work because it offered interaction with other people.

My little Anna was already five years old, and so sweet and sensitive. She grew into a very intelligent and smart kindergartner, and loved me so much. She always made me smile. She also loved Jesus, as much as her nanna.

My friend Roger came to New York, and he invited me out one evening. It was around Christmastime, and we had a lot of fun, looking at the windows of all the shops decorated with Christmas lights. We went to Manhattan, and with him, I saw a part of the city which I had never seen. Roger was always the same, gentle, kind, and a true gentleman. He was the man, who for the first time ever, made me feel like a real person.

In the beginning of 1995, another surprise was awaiting me. Antonella and Santino had decided to move to Williamsburg, Virginia, a small historic town in Southeastern Virginia. The decision was rather quick, and it threw me into a panic. I was so used to seeing Antonella and Anna at my house every day, what would I do without them? A few days later they packed and left.

I fell into a deep depression again. Some really hard times came over me, until again the Lord brought me out of that depression. Fabio, realizing how sad I was, came back to New York. But only for a while, then he too moved to Virginia. I was happy. At least the two brothers would be close together.

My life was running smoothly. There were still problems, but I could deal with them, because I learned to accept God's will. In September, I was shaken by a car accident. I had gone to visit a girlfriend in my car. On the way home, I was hit by a car . The two men in the car didn't even bother to stop.

They drove away laughing. To avoid hitting their car, I had severely damaged a parked car. I sat there, motionless, wondering if the two men had hit me on purpose.

I called the lawyer, and I told him to speed up the divorce proceeding. I would sign whatever Vito wanted, as long as we could get a final divorce soon. In the meantime I had put the house up for sale almost a year ago, but nobody had even come to see it. I wanted to move. There were too many bad memories inside that house. The lawyer said that the final meeting would be on December 19. I begged him to see that I did not have to go to court. I did not want to see Vito. Every time I thought that I was over him and that I had forgiven him, something would happen, and I would be back at the early stages of my therapy.

The lawyer agreed, and finally on the nineteenth of December, the divorce was final! Vito let me have the house, which I had to sell before April to pay all the bills. He also would pay me child support for Tony, but would pay no alimony to me.

When I got back home, I was really depressed. I was worried about not being able to sell the house. Then a verse of scripture came to my mind, from Philippians 4:6. It reads, "Do not be anxious about anything, but in everything, by prayer and petition, with thanksgiving, present your requests to God" (NIV).

At that moment, I raised my hands toward heaven, and prayed. Thirty years of my life had come to an end. Before the end of the year, a young couple came to see the house. They liked it right away, and they started the paperwork with the bank. I had no words left to thank God for helping me one more time.

I had to worry about where I would live. My heart was in Long Island where my friends Marisa and Paolina lived. I also knew the city, and I liked not just the city but also the church that my friends attended. So one weekend, Tony and I went looking for a house to buy. Before I left, the Lord gave me a vision of a cute little house, except I could only see the outside. I prayed to find that house. We saw many houses that day, but not the one that God had shown to me.

In February I went to Virginia to visit my sons. Fabio took me house hunting. Before I even got close to one particular house, I knew that it was the one that I had seen in my vision. It was all white, with blue windows and a blue roof. The front yard had lots of flower beds, all colorful and with butterflies everywhere. My heart filled with joy the minute I walked inside the house. It was the house of my dream. It was large, with three bedrooms and three baths, a large living room, dining room, and a spacious kitchen. The walls were white, and the carpet was blue. I looked toward heaven, and I thanked God that I had found the home of my dreams.

Fabio had fallen in love with a young woman he met in Savannah, Georgia. Emily had moved to Williamsburg, Virginia, with him, and they wanted to get married on June 2, 1996. She was a very beautiful girl, with blonde hair and blue eyes. She had a degree in biology, and was very vivacious and lovely. Her parents were from England, and they were a very nice family. From the very first time that Fabio brought Emily over to my house, I liked her. I wanted to move to Virginia in a hurry, and be able to help them plan their wedding.

I was already half packed, but the closing on the house was not done yet. I was brokenhearted because Rocco did not want to move with me to Virginia. He kept saying that he would stay in New York, and rent a little apartment. I tried to convince him to go with me, but he was twenty-two years old and he had the right to live on his own. I gave up trying to convince him. On April 26, 1996, I closed on the house. Three days later I moved to Virginia.

It was not an easy move. I had an especially difficult time leaving all my friends and the church. I was sad to leave all my sisters in Christ, and afraid I might not make new friends. But the thought of the beautiful house, that God had helped me find, gave me comfort.

Rocco had found a little apartment and moved all his things. He did not look at all happy. I convinced him to come to Virginia, at least until Fabio's wedding, and he agreed. The saddest thing of all was leaving my best friend Tonia. We cried together and hugged, and I thanked her for her warm and sincere friendship. Tony could not break away from Michael. They had been together all their lives, and they loved each other very dearly. Tony did not want to leave, and I felt so sorry for him.

On April 29, I arrived in Williamsburg and moved into my new house. I was happy, because I felt the presence of the Lord inside and around the house. The neighbors welcomed me very warmly and made me feel at home right away. Fabio and Emily had found a little home, and they were also fixing it up nicely. I was happy to be able to help them in any way. Emily was a really affectionate girl, and she did her best to keep me in a good mood. My little Anna was happy to have me back, and she wanted to spend a lot of time with me. Santino and Antonella bought a nice house too, and they were also happy.

By the time I got to Virginia, Fabio and Emily had already sent out their wedding invitations, and they informed me that they had also invited Vito. I was sad and told them that if Vito came to the wedding, I would not. Fabio said, "Mama, I know that you cannot stand him, and that he was not a good father to me, but I am still going to invite him. You must see my point," he said. Of course I saw his point, and I asked him to forgive me.

In May I bought myself a new car. What a conquest for me! It was the very first new car that ever belonged to me! I also bought new furniture for the house, so I was truly starting with everything new. God was being really good to me, and was giving me everything, even things I had never asked for. Two days before the wedding, Vito, Giovanna, and Stephen, arrived in Williamsburg and stayed at Santino's house.

The day of the wedding was a wonderful day. Fabio was so handsome, in his dark suit with a flower in the lapel. When I saw him ready to be married, I hugged him tenderly. My baby was now a man. Santino was his best man, and Rocco and Tony were the escorts. I was wearing a gray silk dress with a matching lace jacket and a matching hat. Vito came to the house, and I gave him also a flower for his lapel. He looked rather moved, but did not say anything. Fabio had asked him to behave like a normal family man, at least for one day.

We then rode in the limousine to the church. We got there early, and I asked the priest if I could sing a song for Fabio and Emily, which I had written myself. When the bride arrived, I walked Fabio to the altar. We were followed by all the other people. Little Anna was the flower girl. She looked so cute in the little white dress I had made for her.

The bride came in on her father's arm. She was breathtakingly beautiful in her satin dress decorated with pearls. Emily was very moved, and looked as if she would pass out. She was holding her father's arm very tightly. The church was packed because it was a Sunday, and the regular parishioners were there for their Sunday Mass. Vito was sitting next to me during the whole Mass. Just before the Communion time, the priest called me to sing. I was so nervous, and I prayed to God to give me the strength and the voice.

I dedicated the song to Fabio and Emily, who were very moved. The words of the songs are:

"La Nostra Casa"

Piano & Vocal

Arranged by
D. Michael McDaniel

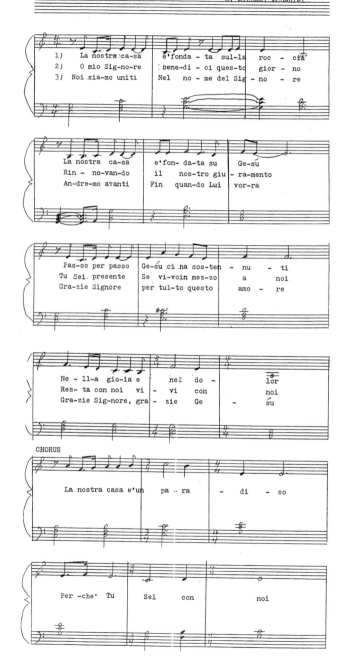

185

The English translation is:

Our house is built on a rock
Our house is built on Jesus.
Step by step Jesus has guided me
in pain and in joy.

Our house is paradise
because you are with me
it will be peaceful and happy
because you are with us.

Oh my Lord, bless this day,
and renew our faith.
You are present, You are alive in our midst
stay with us, live with us.

We are together in the name of the Lord
We will go forward until He so desires
Thank you Lord, for all Your love,
Thank you Lord, thank you Jesus.

When I finished singing, and I went to sit down, I saw that Vito was crying, but he did not say a word.

After the Mass, the newlyweds went to have pictures taken, and we all went to Luigi's, an Italian restaurant. When they came back, we had a very nice reception. Fabio and I danced together, and we both cried. I was so happy and could not believe that another of my sons was now a married man. I always remembered them all as little boys, around my skirt, and slowly they were becoming husbands.

Fabio and Emily left for Jamaica, where they spent their honeymoon. Vito, Giovanna, and Stephen left the day after the wedding. Rocco also went back to New York. Tony and I, our dog Lassie, and our parakeet Noel, settled down in our home. I soon found a wonderful church, Williamsburg Christian Church, where I could serve the Lord and where I taught on Wednesday nights together with a fellow member of the church. I also found a part-time sewing job near my house. I did not make much money, but I enjoyed my work.

During the summer, most of my friends from New York came to visit me in Virginia. Between visits, church, work, and the house, I had a very nice summer. In Williamsburg, I felt at home right away and I had such peace. Rocco came to visit me every couple of months, and he often said that he would move to Virginia someday.

In September Fabio and Emily moved back to Savannah where they both found good jobs, and bought a new home. Santino and Antonella opened a deli together with Antonella's brother-in-law. Its called Avelli Deli. I look forward to working in Santino's deli. I am truly happy, and I hope everything works out for him.

Finally, my life is in order! Although I am alone, I am happy and have peace with myself. My Lord guides me and helps me every single day. Lisa has also become my sister in Christ, which makes me happy. I am sure that slowly, but surely, my whole family will come to know Christ.

As I reflect on my life I realize I have made many wrong turns on my journey for a beautiful life. But along the way I have learned to forgive myself and to forgive others. I have learned to trust the Lord and to walk hand in hand with Jesus. To Him be the praise and glory forever.

My soul finds rest in God alone;
my salvation comes from him.
Psalm 62.1 (NIV)

"Anna Signori Avella" is a pseudonym. The names of all the people and many of the places in this narrative have also been changed. The author has chosen this method in order to spare her children, family, and friends any pain or embarrassment. The words and events in A Springtime's Dream: An Italian Girl's Story are based on the author's true life.

Order Form

Additional copies of this volume may be purchased for
$12.95 plus $3.00 shipping for each book ordered.
(Va. residents add 4.5% sales tax)

Please send _____copies of *A Springtime's Dream* to:

Name _____

Address _____

City _____

State _____

Zip _____

Make checks payable to: **A Springtime's Dream**

Enclosed is a check for _____

($12.95 + $3.00 for each book ordered)

Send Order Form to:

Publishing Connections
P.O. Box 1387
Yorktown, VA 23692-1387